Peng's Complete *of* Treasury

Chinese
Radicals

Peng's Complete Treasury *of* Chinese Radicals

Marshall Cavendish
Editions

Other titles by Tan Huay Peng:
Fun with Chinese Characters Vol. 1, 2 & 3 • *Fun with Chinese Festivals* •
Hanyu Pinyin • *Simplified Chinese Characters* • *What's in a Chinese Character* •
Peng's Complete Treasury of Chinese Idioms

© 2010 Marshall Cavendish International (Asia) Private Limited

This edition is based on *Chinese Radicals Vol. 1 & 2*

Published by Marshall Cavendish Editions
An imprint of Marshall Cavendish International
1 New Industrial Road, Singapore 536196

Other Marshall Cavendish Offices
Marshall Cavendish International. PO Box 65829, London EC1P 1NY, UK •
Marshall Cavendish Corporation. 99 White Plains Road, Tarrytown NY 10591-
9001, USA • Marshall Cavendish International (Thailand) Co Ltd. 253 Asoke, 12th
Flr, Sukhumvit 21 Road, Klongtoey Nua, Wattana, Bangkok 10110, Thailand •
Marshall Cavendish (Malaysia) Sdn Bhd, Times Subang, Lot 46, Subang Hi-Tech
Industrial Park, Batu Tiga, 40000 Shah Alam, Selangor Darul Ehsan, Malaysia

Marshall Cavendish is a trademark of Times Publishing Limited

National Library Board Singapore Cataloguing in Publication Data
Chen, Huoping.
Peng's complete treasury of Chinese radicals / Tan Huay Peng. – Singapore :
Marshall Cavendish Editions, c2010.
p. cm. – (Peng's Chinese treasury)
ISBN-13 : 978-981-4302-41-8

1. Chinese language – Etymology. 2. Chinese language – Word formation.
I. Title. II. Series: Peng's Chinese treasury.

PL1281
495.12 — dc22   OCN559492814

Printed in Singapore by Times Printers Pte Ltd

CHINESE RADICALS

Introduction

Chinese operates differently in many ways from English and other phonetic languages. One of its unique features is that a person having no prior knowledge of Chinese cannot figure out what a Chinese character sounds like from its appearance. With some laboured memory work this initial obstacle may be overcome. Yet an even mightier challenge awaits the learner. Whatever does it mean? A simple yet helpful method of discovering what Chinese characters mean is through studying their radicals.

Chinese dictionaries of old locate characters via stroke count, and by looking under the relevant radical. All Chinese dictionaries have now converted to the Hanyu Pinyin system of reference. Although the function of radicals as dictionary classification is now obsolete, the value of learning about radicals still stands. From a knowledge of them – there exist a total of 214 radicals – a better understanding of those strange composites known as Chinese characters is within reach.

Radicals, or 'root elements', are the foundation of all Chinese characters. They act as common denominators which the mind commits to memory when sizing up the character. Each Chinese character is listed under a particular radical.

Examples

土

The 'earth' radical

欠

The 'yawn' radical

日

The 'sun' radical

心

The 'heart' radical

Identifying the radical

Apart from the previous examples, where the radicals are recognised without difficulty, there are others which are not as easy to identify. Which, for instance, is the radical in 歸? As this character is made up of several elements, a few possibilities are present. However, it is found under the 止 radical. Where there are variant forms of radicals, things get even more complicated. The radical in 舒 is 舌, and the radical in 慕 is 心. 舍 and 小 are both variant forms.

Examples

幫 巾
之 ノ
事 亅
南 十
更 曰
舊 臼
將 寸
成 戈
巨 工
疏 疋
爭 爪
裏 衣

Position of radicals

Neither does the radical always remain in the same position for each of its character examples. Take these characters, which all share the same radical, 口 , the 'mouth' radical.

Characters which function as radicals

About 80 per cent of the radicals also function independently as characters, some examples being:

火 木 車 馬 力 欠

火 , fire, in its capacity as a radical, gives rise to countless other characters which bear a relationship to fire or burning.

炸 烽 烈　燒 燈 煎
熄 炎 熊 煩 煮 炒 照
烘 然　熱

山 , mountain, produces characters referring to hills and mountains and also to height.

岸 島 峽 峰 峻 岡 崩 岳
峨 巒 峭 巖 嶙 嶺 岔 嶄

Classification

In instances where both elements are radicals, the character would be classified under the radical which determines the meaning.

For the character 悶 , both 門 and 心 are radicals. The 心 radical, from whence emotions and feelings arise, is thus the one under which the character is listed.

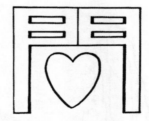

Then again, take a character like 酒 . Both 氵 and 酉 are radicals, but 酉 , meaning 'wine', provides the dominant meaning. The character is therefore found under the 'wine' radical.

Clues to meaning

Radicals are not mere decorative elements. Obviously, in characters which are otherwise purely phonetic, the radical plays the vital role of furnishing the meaning.

hú **湖** (lake)   hú **蝴** (as in butterfly)

liè **烈** (raging)   liè **裂** (split)

Of course there will be cases where the radical plus the other element contribute equally to meaning. The result of combining the 'man' radical with the character for 'word' creates the character 信, trust or believe. Similarly, 証 brings together the 'speech' radical and the character meaning 'correct', resulting in 'prove' or 'testify'.

Telling radicals apart

Some of the radicals are extremely similar in appearance. Avoid confusing these:

Radical 74　月　(moon)
Radical 130　月　(flesh)　　The variant form of 肉.

Radical 72　日　(sun)
Radical 73　曰　(say)

Radical 170　阝　(mound)　Located on the left.
Radical 163　阝　(city)　　Located on the right.

Radical 15　冫　(ice)
Radical 85　氵　(water)　　The variant form of 水.

Radical 27　厂　(cliff)
Radical 53　广　(lean-to)
Radical 104　疒　(disease)

Radical 8　亠　(cover)
Radical 40　宀　(roof)
Radical 116　穴　(cave)

Radical 22　匚　(basket)
Radical 23　匸　(box)

Radical 113　礻　(sign)
Radical 145　衤　(clothes)

Radical 169　門　(door)
Radical 191　鬥　(fight)

Simplified radicals

Radicals which have been simplified are listed below:

Radical 90	爿 → 丬
Radical 147	見 → 见
Radical 149	言 → 讠
Radical 154	貝 → 贝
Radical 159	車 → 车
Radical 167	金 → 钅
Radical 169	門 → 门
Radical 178	韋 → 韦
Radical 181	頁 → 页
Radical 182	風 → 风
Radical 184	食 → 饣
Radical 187	馬 → 马
Radical 191	鬥 → 门
Radical 195	魚 → 鱼
Radical 196	鳥 → 鸟
Radical 197	鹵 → 卤
Radical 199	麥 → 麦
Radical 205	黽 → 黾
Radical 210	齊 → 齐
Radical 211	齒 → 齿
Radical 212	龍 → 龙
Radical 213	龜 → 龟

Effects of simplification

What are some of the repercussions of simplification on radicals?

With evolution into the modern simplified form, some changes have taken place.
E.g., the character for 'pig' does not take for its radical 豕 any more. Other examples supplied here also show a change in radical.

Regular form	Simplified form
豬	猪
牆	墙
範	范
護	护
獲	获
雞	鸡
節	节
驚	惊
黴	霉
體	体
響	响
鹽	盐
葉	叶
願	愿
莊	庄

Even more drastic is the fact that some radicals have vanished altogether.

Regular form   **Simplified form**

開 術 雲 滷   开 术 云 卤

Each of the 214 historical radicals will be enumerated in the complete radical index on pages 20 to 24, and it includes the radical number, variant form, meaning, and one character example.

Because some radicals provide too few or too obscure character examples, it is not possible to analyse each of the 214 radicals individually. Those highlighted warrant attention due to the many useful characters built upon them. An average of 12 examples are given for the major radicals like 'water', 'wood', 'man', 'door', 'speech', etc. For those radicals with fewer relevant examples, an average of 4 have been chosen. Simplifications can be found within brackets.

An explanation follows each character example. Many of these have a whole range of definitions. As the Chinese language is a highly versatile one, a single character very often bears usages and contexts beyond the most obvious and familiar meaning, which is more often than not also the one directly connected to the radical.

Radicals Vol. 1 deals with those radicals which fall under classifications of man, animal, plant and nature, while Vol. 2 carries on with artifacts and implements of man, his actions and characteristics, and finally, numerals and basic strokes.

The Appendix gives a listing of various groups of characters with similar components but different radicals. At a glance it can be seen that with the substitution of a different radical, the character assumes at once a meaning related to it. The listings are by no means exhaustive, and the reader is encouraged to look for other examples, either through the help of the dictionary, or from characters already known.

What to expect

What needs to be stressed at this point is that the radical system is not always the most systematic that one may expect. As there is no hard and fast rule, irregularities do occur. So there should not be too many hairs split over why 辨 comes under the radical 辛 and yet 瓣 is found under the radical 瓜 .

Another area of complexity is where a character having no apparent connection to the radical is nevertheless listed under it! All these defy analysis and have, alas, to be accepted as the freaks of lexicography.

RADICAL INDEX

No.		Pinyin	Meaning	Example
1	一	yī	one	下
2	丨			中
3	丶			主
4	丿			之
5	乙	yǐ		乾
6	亅		hook	事
7	二	èr	two	些
8	亠		cover	亮
9	人(亻)	rén	man	住
10	儿		man (legs)	兄
11	入	rù	to enter	內
12	八	bā	eight	其
13	冂		borders	再
14	冖		crown	冠
15	冫		ice	凍
16	几	jī	table	凱
17	凵		bowl	凶
18	刀(刂)	dāo	knife	割
19	力	lì	strength	動
20	勹		wrap	包
21	匕		ladle	化
22	匚		basket	匠
23	匸		box	匹
24	十	shí	ten	升
25	卜	bǔ	divine	卦
26	卩		seal	印
27	厂		cliff	原
28	厶		cocoon	去
29	又	yòu	right hand	友
30	口	kǒu	mouth	喊
31	囗		enclosure	圍
32	土	tǔ	earth	地
33	士	shì	scholar	壽
34	夂		follow	夆
35	夊		slow	夏
36	夕	xī	dusk	夜
37	大	dà	big	奪
38	女	nǚ	woman	娘
39	子	zǐ	son	存
40	宀		roof	宿
41	寸	cùn	inch	對
42	小	xiǎo	little	少

43	尢(尣, 兀)		lame	就
44	尸	shī	corpse	尾
45	屮		sprout	屯
46	山	shān	mountain	岸
47	川(巛)	chuān	river	州
48	工	gōng	work	差
49	己	jǐ	self	巷
50	巾	jīn	cloth	帽
51	干	gān	shield	平
52	幺	yāo	slender	幾
53	广		lean-to	店
54	廴		march	建
55	廾		clasp	弄
56	弋	yì	dart	式
57	弓	gōng	bow	張
58	彐(彑, ⺕)		pig's head	彙
59	彡		streaks	彰
60	彳	chì	step	從
61	心(忄, 㣺)	xīn	heart	急
62	戈	gē	lance	戰
63	戶	hù	door	房
64	手(扌)	shǒu	hand	提
65	支	zhī	branch	支
66	攴(攵)		knock	放
67	文	wén	literature	爛
68	斗	dǒu	scoop	料
69	斤	jīn	axe	新
70	方	fāng	square	施
71	无	wú	lack	既
72	日	rì	sun	明
73	曰	yuē	to say	會
74	月	yuè	moon	期
75	木	mù	wood	桌
76	欠	qiàn	to yawn	欺
77	止	zhǐ	to stop	步
78	歹	dǎi	bad	殘
79	殳	shū	kill	毀
80	毋(母)		do not!	每
81	比	bǐ	to compare	毗
82	毛	máo	fur	毯
83	氏	shì	clan	民
84	气	qì	breath	氣

85	水(氵，氺)	shuǐ	water	滑
86	火(灬)	huǒ	fire	煮
87	爪(爫)	zhǎo	claw	爭
88	父	fù	father	爸
89	爻	yáo	crisscross	爽
90	爿	bàn	plank	牀
91	片	piàn	slice	版
92	牙	yá	tooth	牚
93	牛(牜)	niú	cow	物
94	犬(犭)	quǎn	dog	獵
95	玄	xuán	dark	率
96	玉(王)	yù	jade	珠
97	瓜	guā	melon	瓠
98	瓦	wǎ	tile	瓶
99	甘	gān	sweet	甜
100	生	shēng	produce	產
101	用	yòng	use	甫
102	田	tian	field	番
103	疋	pī	roll of cloth	疑
104	疒		disease	痛
105	癶		back	發
106	白	bái	white	皇
107	皮	pí	skin	皺
108	皿	mǐn	vessel	盤
109	目	mù	eye	眠
110	矛	máo	spear	矞
111	矢	shǐ	arrow	短
112	石	shí	rock	硬
113	示(礻)	shì	sign	神
114	禸		track	禺
115	禾	hé	grain	種
116	穴	xué	cave	窗
117	立	lì	stand	站
118	竹(⺮)	zhú	bamboo	筆
119	米	mǐ	rice	粒
120	糸		silk	織
121	缶	fǒu	earthenware	罐
122	网(罒，⺳)		net	罪
123	羊(⺶，⺷)	yáng	sheep	羣
124	羽	yǔ	feather	耀
125	老	lǎo	old	考
126	而	ér	yet	耐
127	耒	lěi	plough	耘

128	耳	ěr	ear	聲
129	聿	yù	brush	肆
130	肉(月)	ròu	flesh	脚
131	臣	chén	official	臨
132	自	zì	self	臭
133	至	zhì	reach	致
134	臼	jiù	mortar	舉
135	舌	shé	tongue	舒
136	舛		discord	舞
137	舟	zhōu	boat	船
138	艮	gèn	stubborn	艱
139	色	sè	colour	艷
140	艸(艹)	cǎo	grass	芳
141	虍		tiger	處
142	虫	chóng	insect	蝦
143	血	xuè	blood	蟻
144	行	xíng	go	衝
145	衣(衤)	yī	clothing	裙
146	西(覀)	xī	west	要
147	見	jiàn	see	親
148	角	jiǎo	horn	解
149	言	yán	speech	語
150	谷	gǔ	valley	谿
151	豆	dòu	bean	豐
152	豕	shǐ	pig	象
153	豸	zhì	cat	貌
154	貝	bèi	money	財
155	赤	chì	raw	赦
156	走	zǒu	walk	趕
157	足	zú	foot	跑
158	身	shēn	body	躺
159	車	chē	vehicle	輪
160	辛	xin	bitter	辦
161	辰	chén	time	農
162	辵(辶)		halt	迎
163	邑(阝)	yì	city	部
164	酉		wine	醉
165	釆		separate	釋
166	里	lǐ	mile	野
167	金	jin	gold	鐵
168	長	cháng	long	長
169	門	mén	door	關
170	阜(阝)	fù	mound	院

171	隶		reach	隸
172	隹		short-tailed bird	雄
173	雨	yǔ	rain	雷
174	青	qīng	green	靜
175	非	fēi	not	靠
176	面	miàn	face	靦
177	革	gé	leather	鞋
178	韋	wéi	leather	韓
179	韭	jiǔ	leeks	韮
180	音	yīn	sound	響
181	頁	yè	head	頂
182	風	fēng	wind	颱
183	飛	fēi	fly	飛
184	食	shí	food	餅
185	首	shǒu	chief	馘
186	香	xiāng	fragrance	馥
187	馬	mǎ	horse	騎
188	骨	gǔ	bone	體
189	高	gāo	tall	高
190	髟		hair	鬆
191	鬥	dòu	fight	鬧
192	鬯	chàng	sacrificial wine	鬱
193	鬲		cauldron	鬻
194	鬼	guǐ	demon	魂
195	魚	yú	fish	鮮
196	鳥	niǎo	bird	鵝
197	鹵	lǔ	salt	鹹
198	鹿	lù	deer	麗
199	麥	mài	wheat	麵
200	麻	má	hemp	麼
201	黃	huáng	yellow	黈
202	黍	shǔ	millet	黏
203	黑	hēi	black	默
204	黹	zhǐ	embroider	黼
205	黽	mǐn	try	鼈
206	鼎	dǐng	tripod	鼐
207	鼓	gǔ	drum	鼕
208	鼠	shǔ	mouse	鼯
209	鼻	bí	nose	鼾
210	齊	qí	harmony	齋
211	齒	chǐ	teeth	齡
212	龍	lóng	dragon	襲
213	龜	guī	tortoise	龜
214	龠	yuè	flute	龥

MAN

人	手	彡
儿	又	鬼
女	舌	肉
子	頁	身
口	心	骨
目	足	尸
耳	髟	士

RADICAL 9

rén

man

Of the 214 radicals, one of the most fundamental is the 'man' radical, appearing most often on the left as 亻. Highlighted here are some of the human attributes like health (健), magnificence (偉), handsome countenance (俊), as well as less desirable qualities like pride (傲), stupidity (傻) and treachery (假).

傳(传) chuán
To transfer, to pass on; to circulate.

健 jiàn
Strong, healthy; stout; strengthen, invigorate.

傘(伞) sǎn
Umbrella.

停　tíng
To stop; to halt, to discontinue.

信　xìn
Honest; believe, trust; believe (as in a religion); information; letter.

休　xiū
Rest; retire; stop, give up; do not think; never expect.

修　xiū
Mend, repair; build; edit; study; trim; modify, revise.

佩　pèi
To wear; to respect; to remember.

付　fù
Pay, give to, deliver, hand over.

偉（伟）wěi
Great, magnificent.

傷（伤）shāng
Injury, wound; harm, hurt.

傻　shǎ
Stupid, foolish; stunned, stupefied.

儿

man (legs)

RADICAL 10

Man, besides 人 or 亻, is also depicted by his 2 legs, 儿. Unfortunately, the characters do not all convey the meaning in a defined way, except for 兒, actually a pictograph of an undeveloped brain supported by 2 legs.

光

兢 jīng
Cautious, anxious.

兒(儿) ér
A child, an infant; son; a person.

兄 xiōng
Elder brother; form of polite address.

充 chōng
To fill, to satisfy, to fulfil; to act as.

兇(凶) xiōng
Bad, evil; cruel, savage, ferocious.

先 xiān
First, early; ahead.

光 guāng
Light; glory; scenery; smooth; finished; merely; radiant, naked.

克 kè
Can, able to; to overcome.

免 miǎn
To get rid of; to prevent, not allowed to.

元 yuán
Beginning, first; chief; a unit of currency.

允 yǔn
Promise, consent, approve, allow; fair, appropriate.

兌 duì
Barter; exchange.

女

nǚ

woman

女

RADICAL 38

The 'female' radical naturally appears in the characters for wife, old lady, sister, aunt and other female relatives. One other category is in the characters pertaining to marriage, e.g., 婚 , 嫁 , 娶 , 媒 , 姻; to marry is either to add a woman to the home (嫁) or to obtain a woman (娶)!

好

好 hǎo
Good; fine; friendly; completed; easy.

婚 hūn
Wed; marriage.

妙 miào
Excellent, wonderful; mysterious, subtle.

娶

婆 pó
Old woman; husband's mother.

娶 qǔ
Marry (referring to the man).

姿 zī
Looks, appearance; posture, gesture.

媒 méi
Go-between, matchmaker; a medium, an intermediary.

婦

威 wēi
Intimidating power, might, majesty; coerce, threaten, intimidate.

妥 tuǒ
Good, well-arranged; sound, proper.

嫁

婦（妇）fù
Wife; married woman; daughter-in-law; a female.

嫁 jià
Marry (referring to the woman).

嫩 nèn
Delicate; tender; inexperienced.

子 zǐ

son

RADICAL 39

Although the 'son' radical does not appear in a large number of characters, the characters which bear the 'son' radical suggest life. There is 存 (exist), 孵 (hatch), 孕 (to be with child), 孫 (denoting continuity of the generations). 孝 (filial piety), 學 (study or learn) and 字 (word or character) belong here too.

孝

孜 zī
Diligent; unwearied.

孺 rú
Child; baby.

孔 kǒng
A hole, an opening, an aperture.

孤

存 cún
To exist; to preserve, to keep.

孤 gū
Orphan; solitary.

孩 hái
Child; infant.

季 jì
Season; the youngest of brothers.

孟 mèng
First in order of sons.

學

孫(孙) sūn
Grandchild.

孝 xiào
Filial piety.

學(学) xué
Learn, study; imitate; branch of learning; school.

孕 yùn
Pregnant; generate, breed.

字

字 zì
A word; a written character.

孵 fū
Hatch.

kǒu

mouth

RADICAL 30

The mouth busies itself in many ways – weeping, sighing, shouting, tasting, drinking, asking, informing, grumbling, biting, and not forgetting kissing. These actions are represented in some of the large number of characters with the 'mouth' radical. Put 'mouth' and 'wood' together and the character for 'dumbfounded' – literally, wooden-mouthed – is conceived.

告

呆 dāi
Foolish, stupid; stay.

告 gào
Inform; sue; announce.

喧 xuān
Talk loudly; clamour.

呼吸 hūxī
Breathe; respirate.

吻

哭　kū
To cry, to wail, to weep.

吞　tūn
To swallow; to take possession of.

吻　wěn
Lips; kiss.

喜

喜　xǐ
Joy; pleasure.

hūan
_喜欢_
JOY

商　shāng
Discuss; trade, business; merchant.

喉嚨(喉咙)　hóulóng
Throat, gullet.

嘗(尝)　cháng
To taste, to test; already, formerly.

呆

噴(喷)　pēn
To spurt, to squirt, to sprinkle.

品　pǐn
Goods; articles.

啞(哑)　yǎ
Dumb.

命　mìng
Life; command; fate, destiny.

mù

eye ? See Next pg

RADICAL 109

Whether it is to stare (瞪) or to get some shut-eye (睡), or be hoodwinked by someone (瞞), these are all ways of seeing (or not seeing) and are characters derived from the radical for 'eye'.

睬

睬 cǎi
To bother; to notice; to care for.

眯 mī
Narrow one's eyes; squint.

睜 zhēng
To open eyes wide.

瞒

瞪 dèng
Stare; glare.

瞭(了) liǎo
Understand.

瞒(瞞) mán
Deceive; hoodwink.

盲 máng
Blind.

眉 méi
Eyebrow.

睡

省 shěng
Economize; omit.

睡 shuì
Sleep.

瞎 xiā
Blind.

眼 yǎn
Eye.

省

盼 pàn
To hope; to long for, to look forward to.

瞧 qiáo
Look, see.

相 xiāng
Mutual, reciprocal.

ěr

ear

RADICAL 128

耳

The 'ear' radical is inextricably connected to the faculty of hearing, this being evident in the following examples: deaf (聾), sound (聲), listen (聽), news (聞), which literally means putting the ear to a door. As for intelligence (聰), the meaning is inferred. The ability to grasp ideas quickly through listening leads to comprehension which in turn leads to intelligence.

聲

聵 (聩) kuì
Deaf.

聒 guō
Noisy; clamour, uproar.

聆 líng
Hear; pay attention to.

聯

聰（聪）cōng
Intelligent, clever; alert.

耽 dān
Delay; impede; indulge in.

聚 jù
Assemble; gather, collect.

聯（联）lián
Unite; join; a couplet.

聽

聾（聋）lóng
Deaf; hard of hearing.

聲（声）shēng
Sound; music; voice.

聳（耸）sǒng
Excite, shock; lofty.

聽（听）tīng
Hear, listen; to obey.

聞

聞（闻）wén
Hear; news; smell.

職（职）zhí
Duty; position.

聊 liáo
Depend on; chat.

聖（圣）shèng
Holy; sacred, divine; an imperial decree.

手 shǒu

hand

RADICAL 64

手

Familiarly known in Chinese as 手字旁, the extremely common 'hand' radical denotes a variety of actions executed by the hand. These will include, to mention a few, characters for feel, embrace, seize, scratch, wag, shake, pick, button, copy, point, raise, drag, and countless others.

拜

拜 bài
To pay respects, to visit; to worship.

抱 bào
Embrace, hug; to surround; to cherish.

擋（挡）dǎng
Obstruct, hinder; cover, keep off.

搶 qiǎng
Rob; loot; snatch.

搶

搖 yáo
Shake; sway; flutter; wag.

抓 zhuā
Seize; scratch; arrest, catch.

掌 zhǎng
Palm; control.

描

抖 dǒu
Tremble, shiver.

掛(挂) guà
Hang up, suspend; think of, worry; register.

探 tàn
To search, to explore; to investigate; to visit.

播 bō
To sow, to scatter; to spread, to broadcast.

擋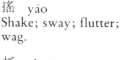

描 miáo
Trace; draw; sketch.

摸 mō
Feel; touch; grope for.

扣 kòu
To hook on; to fasten; to reduce.

又 yòu

right hand

RADICAL 29

The right hand can be used to offer friendship (友), to turn against (反), obtain (取), and bear suffering (受). A force to contend with, certainly.

友 yǒu
Friend; friendly, cordial.

反 fǎn
Contrary, opposite; turn; against; on the contrary.

取 qǔ
Take, get; receive, obtain; choose, use.

受 shòu
Bear, endure; suffer.

shé

tongue

RADICAL 135

舍

The selection of characters from the 'tongue' radical reveals that they are not all related to the tongue, or to licking and tasting. In fact, strangely enough, the variation is 舍 , which does not explain the connection either.

舔

舍 shè
House; hostel.

舐 shì
Lick.

舒 shū
Spread out; stretch.

舔 tiǎn
Lick; taste.

頁 (页)

yè

head

It is the head which controls actions; thus, characters stemming from this radical are significantly those meaning support (頂), lead (領), attend to (顧), and various parts of the head including the neck. One of the changes made through simplification is the change of radical – 顧 becomes 愿 – wishes and desires originate from the heart rather than the head.

頂(顶)　dǐng
The top; the crown of the head; to support; against; argue against; bear; very, extreme.

題(题)　tí
A subject; a topic; a theme.

顧(顾)　gù
Look around; care for, attend to, look after.

顧

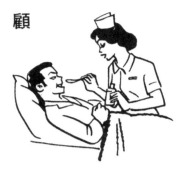

領

額

順(顺) shùn
In the same direction; follow; at one's convenience; arrange; obey; favourable, suitable.

頌(颂) sòng
Praise, commend, admire; psalm.

領(领) lǐng
The neck; the collar; lead, direct; receive.

頸(颈) jǐng
The neck.

願(愿) yuàn
Be willing; wish, desire, hope.

頓(顿) dùn
Pause briefly; immediately; rearrange; stamp; a time.

須(须) xū
Ought, should, must, have to.

額(额) é
The forehead; a fixed number or quantity; a board with an inscription.

xīn

heart

RADICAL 61

Emotions which oftentimes consume man, like fear, hatred, boredom, frustration, regret, shame, misery as well as more positive emotions of benevolence, admiration, forgiveness, loyalty, have their root in the 'heart' radical. It is interesting that 性 (nature) and 慣 (habit), following the dictates of the heart, belong here too.

愁

慰 wèi
Console, comfort.

想 xiǎng
Think; hope; suppose.

慣（惯）guàn
Habitual, accustomed to, used to; pamper.

慚愧 cánkuì
Ashamed.

情 qíng
Emotions, feelings, mood; passion; condition.

惨(惨) cǎn
Miserable, wretched; cruel; seriously.

愁 chóu
Worry.

恩 ēn
Benevolence; kindness.

怒

忍

忍 rěn
Endure; suffer; hard-hearted, cruel.

恕 shù
Forgive, pardon, excuse.

忠 zhōng
Faithful; loyal, devoted.

忠

闷 mèn
Frustrated, unhappy; shut in, stuffy.

怒 nù
Angry, furious; raging.

忧(忧) yōu
Worry, grieve, be anxious about; distress, grief.

zú

foot

RADICAL 157

To kneel (跪) and kick (踢), stride (跨), step upon (踏), trample (踩), jump (跳), follow (跟), fall (跌), run (跑), walk stealthily (蹑) – not surprisingly, the characters for all these actions come under the 'foot' radical.

踢

躍（跃） yuè
Jump.

踐（践） jiàn
Trample, step on.

蹲 dūn
Crouch; squat.

躄 bì
Lame; crippled.

跪

跌 diē
Stumble; slip; decline.

跟 gēn
To follow; with.

跪 guì
Kneel; drop on one's knees.

跨

跨 kuà
Stride; step over; to cross.

路 lù
Road, route; direction, way.

躡(蹑) niè
Walk softly.

跑 pǎo
Run.

蹺

蹺 qiāo
Lift up; raise.

踏 tà
Trample, tread.

踢 tī
Kick.

跳 tiào
To jump; to leap; to beat; to palpitate.

髟

hair

RADICAL 190

Anything hairy – in the form of twirly moustaches, neatly coiled buns, flowing tresses, bristly beards, even the odd toupee or wig – take the 'hair' radical. 鬆 (loose) probably started out to mean hair which has been loosened; the character has however broadened its usage and means 'loose' generally.

髭

鬈 quán
Curly hair.

髭 zī
Moustache.

鬣 liè
Fur.

髮

鬢（鬓）bìn
Curls; hair on the temple.

髮（发）fà
Hair.

鬚（须）xū
Beard.

鬟

髦 máo
Hair on forehead; eminent.

鬟 huán
A round knot of hair worn by Chinese women in the ancient days.

髻
卷

髻 jì
Hair in bun or coil.

鬍（胡）hú
Beard; moustache.

鬆（松）sōng
Loose; relaxed, lenient.

streaks

RADICAL 59

Meaning 'streaks' or 'stripes', this radical only has a handful of characters listed under it. Among these are the characters for 'shape', 'shadow', 'reflection' and 'colour'.

影

影 yǐng
Shadow; image;
reflection.

形 xíng
Shape; appearance.

彬 bīn
Ornamental; refined.

彩 cǎi
Colours; spirit or
energy of mind.

鬼

RADICAL 194

guǐ

demon

鬼

All things demonic and ghostly come under the 'demon' or 'devil' radical. These naturally include the characters for demon, spirit or soul. Incidentally, to have 魔力 (charm or attraction) is to possess bewitching powers!

魔

魂 hún
Spirit; soul.

魁 kuí
Chief; great, eminent; well-built.

魔 mó
Devil, demon; bewitching, fascinating.

魄 pò
Soul; vigour; spirit.

ròu

flesh

月

RADICAL 130

Though the 'flesh' radical mostly appears as 月, it should not be mistaken for the 'moon' radical. Rather, most of the characters specify different parts of the body, or the state of rotundity (肥), swelling of the flesh (腫), exposure of it (脫), and other manifestations.

背

背 bèi
Back; the reverse; to learn by heart.

膚(肤) fū
Skin; surface; shallow, superficial.

臉(脸) liǎn
Face; expression.

腰

脱 tuō
Strip; peel.

膽(胆) dǎn
Gall; courage.

腰 yāo
Waist; loins.

腿 tuǐ
Legs and thighs.

胃 wèi
Stomach.

腫(肿) zhǒng
Swell.

腫

肩 jiān
Shoulder; to shoulder
(responsibility).

腐 fǔ
Rotten, decay, spoilt.

胖 pàng
Fleshy; fat.

能 néng
Capability; talent, skill;
able.

胖

胸 xiōng
Chest, thorax; outlook,
mind.

肺 fèi
The lungs.

shēn

body

RADICAL 158

Characters from the 'body' radical are very few indeed, but do describe the body (軀) per se, in a reclining position (躺), in a bending position (躬), or in a hidden position (躲).

躲

躲 duǒ
Conceal; hide away.

躬 gōng
Body; personally; bend.

軀 (躯) qū
Human body.

躺 tǎng
Lie down.

RADICAL 188

gǔ

bone

Bones provide the framework and structure to the body, so in the same way the 'bone' radical consists of characters like 體 (body) and 骯髒 (dirty).

骯髒

骯髒（肮脏） āngzāng
Dirty, filthy.

體（体） tǐ
The body, the trunk; the substance, the essence; the form, the system.

shī

corpse

RADICAL 44

This radical has the unusual meaning of 'corpse'. However, characters belonging to it have no real association with cadavers or corpse-like objects. They are as diverse as dwell, house, urine, tail, department, drawer, etc. Simply defies explanation!

居

展 zhǎn
Open; launch; to postpone, to extend; to exhibit.

屋 wū
House.

屈 qū
Bend; submit.

屋

尿

尾

層（层） céng
Layer; storey.

居 jū
Dwell; occupy.

局 jú
Office, bureau,
department; condition.

屉 tì
Drawer; tray.

屬（属） shǔ
Class, category; belong.

尿 niào
Urine.

屑 xiè
Bits and pieces,
fragments; petty, trivial.

尾 wěi
Tail; ending.

屠 tú
To butcher, to kill, to
slaughter.

屏 píng
Screen.

shì

scholar

RADICAL 33

Clustered under the 'scholar' radical are a surprising group of characters, from 壺 (pot or kettle) to 壯 (strong or robust – in character or physique) to 壽 (longevity), one of the Three Abundances seen symbolically in many Chinese crafts.

壯

壯(壮) zhuàng
Strong, robust, stout.

壺(壶) hú
A pot; a kettle.

壽(寿) shòu
Life, age; longevity; birthday.

ANIMAL

牛	豸	隹
馬	虍	羽
犬	虫	毛
豕	魚	革
羊	鳥	鹿

牛

niú

cow

RADICAL 93

牛

A humble farm animal, the beast of burden, the 'cow' is the radical for several characters, among which the more interesting are 牽 (to lead), 牢 (cattle-pen or prison), and the fact that these latter meanings share the same character is probably accountable to the similarity between the jail and a cattlepen! Being in jail is equivalent to being a cow in a stable.

牢

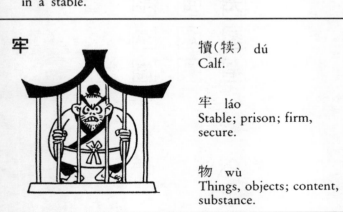

犢（犊） dú
Calf.

牢 láo
Stable; prison; firm, secure.

物 wù
Things, objects; content, substance.

牲

牲 shēng
Livestock.

特 tè
Special; extraordinary.

犧牲（牺牲） xīshēng
Sacrifice.

牧

犖（牢） luò
Clear.

牧 mù
To pasture, tend; herd.

犂 lí
To plough; a plough.

犀 xī
Rhinoceros.

牽

牽（牵） qiān
Pull; drag, haul; lead.

牡 mǔ
Male (birds, animals).

牝 pìn
Female (of birds or animals).

馬 （马）

mǎ

horse

RADICAL 187

Horse power is the driving force behind these characters. Modes of transport like the horse carriage of yore gave rise to 駕, meaning drive. Thankfully, the character 駕 has not become obsolete though the horse carriage is no longer a common sight along city thoroughfares. Wild horses also need to be tamed, resulting in 馴. 'Horse' is one of the more important animal radicals.

 **駝**

駄（驮） tuó
To carry on the back.

驢（驴） lǘ
Donkey.

馱（驮） duò
A load, a burden.

駛（驶） shǐ
Drive, steer; to speed.

驚

駕（驾）jià
Ride; drive; control; yoke.

驚（惊）jīng
Terrify; frighten; surprise.

騙（骗）piàn
Swindle; cheat.

駝（驼）tuó
Camel; hunchbacked.

騰（腾）téng
To mount, to soar; to jump; to vacate.

騾（骡）luó
Mule.

騎

騎（骑）qí
Ride.

馴

驅（驱）qū
To urge, to drive; to drive away, to expel.

馴（驯）xún
Tame, docile; domesticate, subdue.

驗（验）yàn
To inspect, to examine; effective.

犬

RADICAL 94

quǎn

dog

犭

Functioning as a radical, 'dog' exhibits the fiercer side of its nature. Apparently the dog's ferocity determines characters like 猛 (fierce), 犯 (violate), 狂 (violent). 犭 is also the radical for a whole menagerie of animals like gorilla (猩), lion (獅), fox (狐狸), wolf (狼), monkey (猴) and gibbon (猿).

獄

獵 (猎) liè
Hunting.

狼 láng
Wolf.

狂 kuáng
Mad; eccentric; violent; wild.

犯

独（独） dú
Solitary, single, alone.

状（狀） zhuàng
Appearance, shape, condition.

犯 fàn
Violate; offend; invade; infringe; commit.

猴

狮（獅） shī
Lion.

獣（獸） shòu
Animal; beast.

狱（獄） yù
Prison, jail; law suit.

猜 cāi
To guess.

狡 jiǎo
Crafty, cunning, sly.

猛 měng
Strong; violent; brave; fierce; suddenly.

献（獻） xiàn
Present; offer; contribute.

猴 hóu
Monkey.

狂

shǐ

pig

RADICAL 152

As a radical, 'pig' is not very significant, and it concerns rather few characters. About the most remarkable character from the list happens to be 象 (elephant). Whatever the connection is between pig and elephant remains to be discovered!

豕

豬（猪）zhū
A pig, a hog, a swine.

豢 huàn
To feed (livestock); to cherish (henchmen).

豚 tún
A piglet or a pig.

豪豬（豪猪）háozhū
A porcupine.

羊

RADICAL 123

yáng

sheep

￿ ￿

Despite the fact that the 'sheep' radical is not featured in many characters, it is nevertheless responsible for characters representing the virtues of beauty (美), justice (義), admiration (羨) and meekness (羞); though whether meekness is considered a virtue depends entirely on the situation at hand.

羞

羨 xiàn
Admire; envy.

羣(群) qún
Crowd; group; flock.

羞 xiū
To feel ashamed; shy.

羚 líng
Antelope, gazelle.

義(义) yì
Justice; righteousness.

zhì

reptile

RADICAL 153

This radical actually means reptile, except that the characters associated with it are not reptilean in resemblance, but those belonging to the cat family, such as the sable (貂), leopard and panther (豹), and the domestic cat.

豹 bào
A leopard; a panther; a species of wild cat.

豺 chái
A ravenous beast, akin to jackal.

貂 diāo
The sable; the marten.

貌 mào
Face; appearance.

虍

RADICAL 141

tiger

Under the 'tiger's head' radical come a number of absolutely diverse characters, the more common examples being empty (虛), lose (虧), place (處), and sign or number (號).

虐

虧（亏） kuī
Lose; deficient; thanks to, owing to.

號（号） hào
Name; sign; number.

虛 xū
Empty, vacant; false; weak; humble.

虐 nüè
Harsh, cruel, tyrannical.

chóng

insect

The insect kingdom, with its many different species, is revealed in the character examples from the 'insect' radical. However, apart from the usual creepy crawlies like ants (螞蟻), lizard (蜥蜴), cockroach (蟑螂), there are the winged creatures like the dragonfly (蜻蜓), butterfly (蝴蝶), firefly (螢火蟲), and sea creatures like crab (螃蟹) and prawn (蝦).

蝴蝶

蝴蝶　húdié
Butterfly.

蝙蝠　biānfú
Bat.

螞蟻（蚂蚁）　máyǐ
Ants.

蟲（虫）　chóng
A worm, an insect.

蟲

蜜

螢

融 róng
To melt; to dissolve, to thaw; to reconcile.

蚯蚓 qiūyǐn
Earthworm.

蠟(蜡) là
Wax; paraffin; bees-wax.

蜜 mì
Honey; sweet.

螃蟹 pángxiè
Crab.

螢(萤) yíng
Firefly.

蠢 chǔn
Stupid, sluggish.

蛋 dàn
An egg.

蜘蛛 zhīzhū
Spider.

蛇 shé
Snake.

蜻蜓 qīngtíng
Dragonfly.

魚 （鱼）

yú

fish

RADICAL 195

The function of the 'fish' radical is obvious, but it must be noted that the whale, though a mammal, also takes 'fish' for its radical because of its fish-like appearance. Also, the character for fresh (鮮) comes under the 'fish' radical as well. Fish is always expected to be fresh; stale fish smells and tastes dreadful!

鯧（鲳） chāng
A pomfret.

鰭（鳍） qí
Fins of fish.

鱗（鳞） lín
Scales (of fish, reptile, etc.)

鯊

魯（鲁）lú
Dull, stupid; rude, rough.

鮮（鲜）xiān
Fresh; bright, colourful.

鯊（鲨）shā
Shark.

鯨（鲸）jīng
Whale.

鯿（鳊）biān
Carp.

鰓（鳃）sāi
The gills of fish.

鰻（鳗）mán
Eel.

鱉（鳖）biē
Freshwater turtle.

鯁（鲠）gěng
Bone of fish.

鮑（鲍）bào
Abalone.

鱷魚（鳄鱼）èyú
Crocodile.

鯨

鯁

鳥 （鸟）　niǎo

bird

Practically the whole of fowl life is represented by examining the 'bird' radical – from the humble duck (鴨) to the more exotic varieties like flamingo (紅鶴), crane (鶴), and the mythical phoenix (鳳).

鶴

鴉（鸦）　yā
The crow.

鴿（鸽）　gē
Dove; pigeon.

鴻（鸿）　hóng
Wild swan; huge, great.

鳳

鵝（鹅）é
Domestic goose; swan.

鳳（凤）fèng
Phoenix.

鶉（鹑）chún
Quail.

鷓（鹧）zhè
The common partridge.

鴛（鸳）yuān
Male mandarin duck.

鷹（鹰）yīng
Eagle; falcon; hawk.

鵬（鹏）péng
Fabulous bird of
enormous size – the roc.

鴨

鴨（鸭）yā
Duck.

鸚（鹦）yīng
Parrot.

鶴（鹤）hè
A crane; a stork.

你好吗！

鸚

隹

RADICAL 172

short-tailed bird

This radical means 'short-tailed bird' as in sparrow (雀) and chicken (雞). 集 actually is a pictograph of a bird perched on a tree, and now means a gathering or assembly; similarly, 雙 depicts 2 birds in the hand and signifies a pair.

集

雁 yàn
Wild goose.

雍 yōng
Harmonious; dignified.

雇 gù
Employ, hire, engage.

雕 diāo
Eagle; engrave.

雛(雏) chú
A young bird.

雜(杂) zá
Miscellaneous, assorted.

雄 xióng
A strong and powerful
person, a hero; majestic,
magnificent.

離(离) lí
Depart, leave; lack;
from.

雖(虽) suī
Although.

雀 què
Sparrow; small birds in
general.

集 jí
Assemble; accumulate.

雅 yǎ
Elegant, refined.

難(难) nán
Difficult.

雙(双) shuāng
A pair; double.

羽

RADICAL 124

yǔ

feather, wing

Whereas Radical 82 is 毛, which could be 'fur' or 'feather', 羽 only refers to 'feather' or 'plumage'. Of the examples given the most outstanding is 耀 – a composite of brightness, feathers and bird. Imagine a bird showing off its fine plumage, hence 'glory'.

不倒翁

翔 xiáng
Soar; hover over.

翎 líng
A plume; a feather.

翹(翘) qiào
To elevate, to raise.

翁　wēng
Old man; father-in-law;
father.

翅　chì
Wings.

習(习)　xí
Practise, revise; habit.

翠　cuì
Bluish-green.

翰　hàn
Brush; literary.

翼　yí
Wings.

翻　fān
Overturn; cross.

耀　yào
Shine brightly; dazzle.

翡　fěi
Kingfisher; jade.

翌　yì
Next.

翕　xì
To unite; together, all.

máo

fur

毛

RADICAL 82

Garments or items made from fur or wool or feather, like carpets, blankets, shuttlecocks, down jackets, etc., appear in the Chinese vocabulary as characters based on the 'fur' radical.

毯

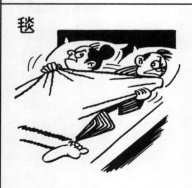

氅 chǎng
Cloak; garment of down.

毽 jiàn
Shuttlecock.

毯 tǎn
Blanket; rug; carpet.

氈(毡) zhān
Felt; fabrics used for rugs, carpets, etc.

gé

leather

RADICAL 177

Just as leather or hide is the material out of which miscellaneous articles like shoes, boots, whips, saddles, etc., are fashioned, the radical for these very same characters is 'leather' or 'hide'.

靴 xuē
Boots.

鞍 ān
A saddle.

鞋 xié
Shoes.

鞭 biān
A whip, a lash.

lù

deer

RADICAL 198

Undoubtedly one of the most elegant and beautiful creatures on four legs, the deer features most fittingly as a radical in 麗. In this other example, 麓 is an ideograph. 'Deer' appearing below 'forest' conveys the idea of foothills.

麗(丽) lì
Beautiful, handsome; splendid.

麓 lù
Foothills.

麒麟 qílín
Fabulous animal of good omen; Chinese unicorn.

PLANT

艸	木	米
竹	禾	豆

cǎo

grass

RADICAL 140

艹

Known also in Chinese as 草字頭 , the 'grass' radical is one of the most important radicals, and incorporates most flora and fauna. There are over 300 examples. Characters which suggest the artistic and elegant (華, 藝) belong here, as does the character for medicine (藥), seeing that traditional Chinese medicine is brewed from herbs.

藝

菊 jú
Chrysanthemum.

華(华) huá
Chinese; splendid, grand; beauty.

薑(姜) jiāng
Ginger.

葱 cōng
Onion; green in colour.

荒

落 luò
Fall; shed; decline; settle upon; a gathering place.

蓋(盖) gài
A cover, a lid; build; affix a seal.

荒 huāng
Uncultivated, wild.

藥

蕭(萧) xiāo
Desolate, barren.

薄 báo
Thin; indifferent, heartless; small.

藝(艺) yì
Skill, craft; art.

藥(药) yào
Medicine; cure, remedy; chemicals.

荷

葉(叶) yè
Leaf.

葡萄 pútáo
Grapes.

荷 hé
Lotus flower; water lily.

藤 téng
Rattan, cane; creepers, climbing plants.

竹

zhú

bamboo

RADICAL 118

To demonstrate the use of the 'bamboo' radical are the characters for screen (簾), fence (籬笆), chopsticks (筷), basket (籃), cage (籠), arrow (箭), and pipe (簫). Many of these items are indeed made from bamboo.

筷

範(范) fàn
A pattern; a model, a standard.

築(筑) zhù
To build, to construct.

篾 miè
Bamboo splints.

籮(箩) luó
Deep and open basket without a cover, made of bamboo.

管 guǎn
A pipe; a flute; govern; supervise.

箏 zhēng
A stringed instrument.

算 suàn
Count, calculate; plan, contrive; consider; reckon.

箭 jiàn
Arrow.

節(节) jié
A knot, a joint; a section, a paragraph; a season; a festival; restrict, economize; a measure word.

簾(帘) lián
A screen, a bamboo-blind.

簫(箫) xiāo
A flute.

籃(篮) lán
Basket.

籬笆(篱笆) líbā
A fence, a hedge (of bamboo).

筷 kuài
Chopsticks.

木

RADICAL 75

mù

wood

Another basic and most versatile radical, the 'wood' element is present in hundreds of characters, a large category being things which could be constructed from wood: table (桌), chair (椅), bridge (橋), beam (梁). 'Wood' is also the radical for different types of trees, like coconut (椰), cotton (棉), willow (柳), or even parts of the tree, such as firewood (柴), roots (根), branches (樹枝), and fruits (呆).

柴

栽 zāi
To cultivate; to tumble; saplings.

槌 chuí
A mallet, a pestle; to strike, to beat.

楚 chǔ
Clear, distinct, orderly; pain.

棋

根

槳

業（业） yè
Business, profession, work; property, estate; to engage in.

棋 qí
Chess.

柱 zhù
Pillar, post, column.

樹（树） shù
Tree; establish.

根 gēn
Roots; foundation; a measure word.

樓（楼） lóu
A house with one or more storeys; an upper floor or storey.

槳（桨） jiǎng
An oar, a paddle.

梁 liáng
A beam; a bridge; an elevation; a ridge.

柴 chái
Firewood.

櫥 chú
A case, a cupboard.

hé

grain

The 'grain' radical is responsible for such characters as 穫 (harvest), 積 (store up), 種 (plant), 穀 (cereal), 稻 (rice, padi). Though the original meanings of 穫 and 積 are related to farming and harvesting and storage of the crop, its more acquisitive and commercial applications may well be left to the imagination.

穫

稻 dào
Padi, rice.

穫(获) huò
Reaping, harvest.

稅 shuì
Tax, duty, toll.

積(积) jī
Accumulate, store up;
gather, hoard.

積

秋

稿

秀 xiù
Beautiful.

私 sī
Selfish; private; secret.

秋 qiū
Autumn; harvest time;
year; a period of time.

科 kē
A classification; a
department, a category;
to sentence; to levy
(taxes).

租 zū
To rent, to lease; rental.

移 yí
Move, shift; change,
transfer.

程 chéng
Regulations, formula; a
journey; procedure.

稱(称) chēng
To estimate, to weigh;
to address; to express.

穀(谷) gǔ
Grain, cereals.

稿 gǎo
The stalk of grain,
straw; manuscript.

米 mǐ

rice

RADICAL 119

米, the 'rice' radical, does not restrict itself to characters like 粥 (porridge), 糖 and 糕 (confections), 粉 (flour), etc. – products derived from a rice base – but is also the radical for 精 (shrewd), 粘 (paste), 糢糊 (muddled).

粉

粉 fěn
Flour; powder; whitewash; grind to a powder; cosmetic powder.

粗 cū
Coarse, thick; unfinished, rough; vulgar, rude.

糟

粒 lì
A grain; a measure word.

糟 zāo
Sediment, grains from a distillery; to decay, to rot; in chaos.

粘 zhān
To paste up, to stick on, to affix.

粘

糧（粮）liáng
Grain, provisions, food.

糕 gāo
Cakes, pastries.

粥 zhōu
Porridge, congee, rice gruel.

糖

糖 táng
Sugar; sweets and candies.

粹 cuì
Pure; essence.

糊 hú
Paste, gum.

精 jīng
Refined; best, exquisite; clever; energy; skilful.

dòu

bean

RADICAL 151

Nowadays numerous products are made from beans. Not many characters belong to the 'bean' radical, but there is one distinctive example close to the heart of many. To have an abundance of riches, food, and life's material comforts – that is to be 豐富 .

豐

豈（岂） qǐ
An interrogative
particle. How?

登 dēng
Ascend, mount; register,
note.

豐（丰） fēng
Graceful; abundant,
plentiful.

NATURE

日	水	厂	石
月	火	土	山
夕	雨	金	穴
風	寸	玉	阜
冫	里	田	邑

日

rì

sun

RADICAL 72

The source of all light and energy and warmth, this is the 'sun', the solar radical. Hence we have characters like 暖 (warm), 映 (shine), 春 (spring – the arrival of sunshiny days after cold dreary winters), 早 (early). 智 (wisdom), quite appropriately, belongs here as well.

暖 nuǎn
Warm, genial.

暫 (暂) zàn
Temporarily, for a short time.

暴 bào
Violent; cruel, tyrannical; to show, to expose; to injure; hot-tempered.

昏

昏 hūn
Evening, dusk; gloomy, dark; faint, lose consciousness; confused.

星 xīng
Star; planet, celestial body.

時(时) shí
Time; season; unit for measuring time as used in ancient China; current; always; sometimes.

晚 wǎn
Night; late.

晨 chén
Morning, dawn, daybreak.

景

景 jǐng
Scenery, sight; situation, circumstances; admire.

晶 jīng
Bright, shining; crystal.

智 zhì
Wisdom, intelligence.

暗

暗 àn
Dark; secret, private; hidden; ignorant.

月

yuè

moon

RADICAL 74

Previous to this the 'flesh' radical was discussed; this then is the 'moon' radical which could be easily mistaken for it if not careful. With its many traditional associations with romance, some of the characters are 朋 (friend), 朦朧 (hazy), and 望 (hope, desire).

朦朧

朦朧(朦胧) ménglóng
Half asleep, drowsy;
dim moonlight; obscure,
hazy.

有 yǒu
Have, possess; to exist;
rich, plentiful.

朋 péng
Friend, acquaintance, companion; a clique; to match, to compare.

服 fú
Clothes; submit, obey; serve, wait upon; take (medicine); be accustomed to.

朔 shuò
The first day of the lunar month; north.

朗 lǎng
Clear, bright; clear and distinct sound.

望 wàng
Look afar; pay a visit; hope, expect; reputation; the fifteenth day of a lunar month.

朝 zhāo
Morning, early; day.

期 qī
A period; hope, expect; make an appointment; issue.

朣 tóng
Dim light; obscure, confused.

xī

夕

dusk

RADICAL 36

At the time when the sun sets and the moon newly appears in the skies – there is always an aura of romance. 夢 (dream) is one of the few characters listed under the 'dusk' radical. Perhaps the most famous dream of all is the Chinese classic, *Dream of the Red Chamber.*

夢

外 wài
Outside, external.

多 duō
Plenty; a great number.

夜 yè
Night.

夠 gòu
Enough, sufficient.

夢（梦） mèng
Dream.

風 （风） fēng
wind

風

RADICAL 182

Winds can either be gentle and light, causing persons and objects to be gently swept up, or else have violent manifestations in the form of hurricanes (颶) or typhoons (颱), leaving more destruction in their wake.

飄

颱（台） tái
Typhoon.

颶（飓） jù
Typhoon; hurricane.

颳（刮） guā
Blow.

飄（飘） piāo
To flutter, to fly; to float about.

> **RADICAL 15**

ice

The 'ice' radical encompasses that which is cold, icy and frozen; that includes delivering the freeze treatment to unsavoury characters . . . For the character 冰, the addition of the 'ice' radical to the character representing water shapes the meaning. Ice, after all, is water in a frozen state.

冰

冽 liè
Very cold, chilly.

冰 bīng
Ice.

凜 lǐn
Cold; stern, severe.

冷

准 zhǔn
Allow, permit; correct, exact.

冷 lěng
Cold, chilly; lonesome, quiet; indifferent; sarcastic; secretly.

凌 líng
Ice; ill-treat; advance; rise, soar.

凝

冶 yě
Smelt; melt; fuse.

凍(冻) dòng
Freeze; frozen, icy.

凋 diāo
Fading, withered, declined, fallen (leaves).

凍

凝 níng
To liquify; to solidify; to concentrate.

冬 dōng
Winter.

水

RADICAL 85

shuǐ

water

氵

Considering that water is one of the four main elements, it is understandable just how many characters have their roots in this radical. Always referred to as 三點水 , 3 drops of water, it can be found in characters for drench, drop, leak, drown, deep, float, damp, bathe, etc. Tears, being in a liquid state, are included too.

涙

濟(济) jì
Help, relieve; cross a river, ferry.

淚(泪) lèi
Tears.

淺(浅) qiǎn
Shallow; easy to understand; superficial; light in colour.

滴 dī
Dripping; trickle, drop.

淋

漏

漂

灣（湾） wān
A bay, a gulf.

游泳 yóuyǒng
Swim.

淋 lín
Drenched; sprinkle.

洲 zhōu
A shoal, a sandbank; an island; the continent.

浪 làng
Waves, breakers; wasteful, dissolute.

泉 quán
Spring water.

漏 lòu
Leak, drip; disclose.

溝（沟） gōu
A creek, a canal; ditch; trench.

濕（湿） shī
Wet, damp.

漂 piāo
To float, to drift.

淹 yān
Drown, immerse, submerge.

huǒ

fire

RADICAL 86

Characters related to burning or heat take as their radical the other main element of 'fire'. Methods of cooking like roasting, baking and frying are examples, as are having a fever (發燒), exploding (爆), scalding (燙), and ash (灰).

燙

爐（炉） lú
A stove, a fireplace, a furnace, an oven.

燙（烫） tàng
Scalding; to iron.

災（灾） zāi
Disaster, calamity.

烟

灰　huī
Ashes, cinder; dust; grey; disheartened.

烤　kǎo
To roast; to bake.

烟　yān
Smoke, fume; cigarette; tobacco.

熄

煤　méi
Coal.

熄　xī
Extinguish, die out.

熟　shú
Cooked; ripe; familiar; deep; processed.

燈(灯)　dēng
A lamp; a lantern; a light.

燒

燒(烧)　shāo
Burn; cook or heat something; roast, bake; fever.

爆　bào
To explode, to crack, burst, scorch.

yǔ

rain

RADICAL 173

Many climatic conditions are represented by characters under the 'rain' radical. The natural phenomena to which man is subject are examples – rain, fog, sleet, hail, thunder, lightning, snow, frost.

雹 báo
Hail.

露 lù
Dew; expose, bare;
made manifest.

靈(灵) líng
Intelligent; effective;
spiritual, supernatural.

雪 xuě
Snow; clean; avenge.

雲(云) yún
Clouds.

雷 léi
Thunder.

電(电) diàn
Electricity.

電

震

需 xū
Need, want, require.

霜 shuāng
Frost; grizzled.

震 zhèn
To shake, to quake, be alarmed.

霞 xiá
Rosy clouds.

霧(雾) wù
Mist, fog.

霖 lín
Continuous heavy rain.

雪

霧 fēn
Mist.

雯 wén
Cloud in beautiful patterns.

cùn

inch

RADICAL 41

Attentiveness and direction can be used to describe the characteristics behind examples of the 'inch' radical. 專 is to direct attention, 導 to guide and direct, 射 to inject or shoot in a certain direction, 尋 to look carefully in all directions.

導

尊 zūn
Honourable, senior; to respect, to honour; a measure word for cannon.

導(导) dǎo
Lead, guide, direct; conduct.

尋

尋(寻) xún
Find, seek, search, look for.

對(对) duì
Opposite; correct; answer; towards; check, examine; a pair.

封 fēng
Close, seal; restrict, limit; a measure word for letter.

射

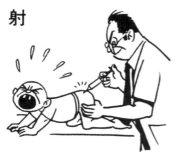

射 shè
Shoot, project; inject; to radiate light or heat.

專(专) zhuān
Single-minded, attentive; specialized, special.

專

將(将) jiāng
Shall, will, soon; presently; get, use.

尉 wèi
An official in ancient China; a rank in the armed forces.

里 lǐ

mile

RADICAL 166

The few characters which the 'mile' radical is responsible for are nonetheless weighty enough to deserve mention. 重, 量 and 野 denote, respectively, weight, quantity and distance.

重

重 zhòng
Heavy; weight; serious; main, important.

野 yě
Wilderness, a moor, countryside; limit, region; rough, uncivil, savage, rude.

量 liàng
A measure, a quantity; capacity; volume, output; think, estimate.

RADICAL 27

cliff

厭 , an example of a character under the 'cliff' radical, means 'loathe' or 'be contemptuous of', almost as if everything is regarded from a great elevation, making things down below seem small and trivial.

厭

原 yuán
Original, initial; crude, raw; a plain.

厭（厌） yàn
Dislike, dissatisfied, be fed up, loathe.

厲（厉） lì
A whetstone; sharpen, grind; stern; cruel, harsh, oppressive.

tǔ

earth

RADICAL 32

The following examples help to demonstrate the relationship between man and earth. First of all it provides a foundation (基), upon which a city (城) can be built. Man can however wreck it (壞), be crushed by it in a landslide (壓), or be buried under it (埋).

埋

埋 mái
To bury; conceal.

堅(坚) jiān
Strong, hard, solid;
determined, resolute.

壘(垒) lěi
A rampart, a fort, a
fortress; build by piling
up (as bricks).

基 jī
Foundation; according
to, based on; basic,
fundamental.

城 chéng
City, town.

塗（涂） tú
To apply, to smear; to
erase, to cross out.

境 jìng
A limit, a boundary;
a place, a region;
situation, circumstances.

墨 mò
Black ink.

墳（坟） fén
A grave.

塵（尘） chén
Dust, dirt; earth.

壓（压） yā
Exert pressure on,
crush; suppress,
overpower with force;
control, restrain; draw
near, close in.

壞（坏） huài
Bad; dilapidated, broken
down.

塞 sè
To block, to fill up.

金 （钅）

jīn

gold

金

RADICAL 167

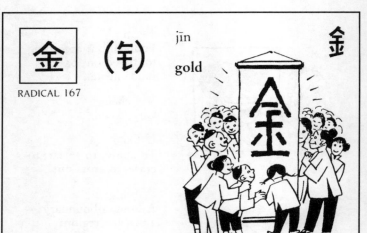

Gold is considered by most people as the most important metal of all, as it connotes wealth and status, and is much coveted. As a radical it has also assumed a metallurgical function. Metals like iron, steel, copper, silver, platinum, etc., bear this radical; so are activities related to metals, such as forge, smelt, drill, chisel, and so on.

錢

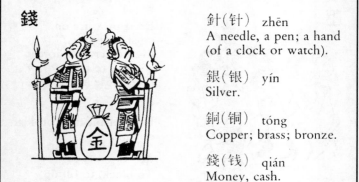

針（针） zhēn
A needle, a pen; a hand (of a clock or watch).

銀（银） yín
Silver.

銅（铜） tóng
Copper; brass; bronze.

錢（钱） qián
Money, cash.

錯

鏡

鑽

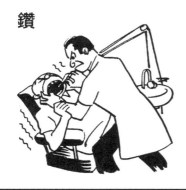

銳（锐） ruì
Sharp.

鋒（锋） fēng
A sharp point, a blade; sharp, acute.

鍛（锻） duàn
Temper; forge.

錯（错） cuò
A mistake, an error; wrong; cross.

鏡（镜） jìng
A mirror, lens.

鏢（镖） biāo
A throwing weapon, a dart.

鐵（铁） tiě
Iron.

鑽（钻） zuān
To bore, to drill; to go into, to penetrate.

鏨（錾） zàn
A chisel.

鈴（铃） líng
A bell (musical); a bell (e.g. door-bell); any bell-like articles.

玉

yù

jade

王

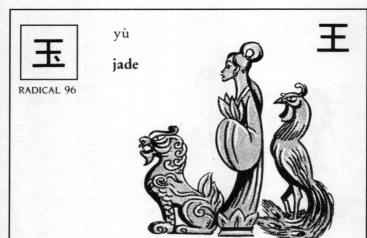

In most cases, the 'jade' radical appears only as 王, the dot being dispensed with. As jade represents precious stones, characters belonging to the radical extend to pearl (珠), coral (珊瑚), agate (瑪瑙), and gems galore, almost as if these were contents of a treasure chest.

珍

珍 zhēn
Precious things, treasure; valuable, excellent; to value and treasure.

理 lǐ
The structure of material; law, principle; manage, undertake; arrange; regulate; acknowledge, heed.

琴

珠

玩

琴 qín
A string instrument, a lute; a general name for some musical instruments like piano, accordion, harmonica.

瑩（莹） yíng
A jade-like stone; shining and transparent.

環（环） huán
Ring, a bracelet; to encircle; around.

珠 zhū
Pearl; beads, drops, or anything else small and round.

珊瑚 shānhú
Coral.

瑪瑙 mǎnǎo
Agate.

璧 bì
A kind of jade.

玻璃 bōlí
Glass.

玩 wán
Play; admire; treat with contempt; trifle with.

tián

field

RADICAL 102

In his traditional role, man is seen as provider by virtue of his sex, and is expected to plough the land and toil in the fields all day while the woman busies herself with domestic chores. Thus the character for 'male' is an ideograph of a field to which strength or energy is applied. The connection of the 'field' radical to other characters is less obvious.

界 jiè
Boundary, a frontier; range, extent, horizon; a world.

畜 xù
Rear animals, breed livestock.

留 liú
Stay, remain; pay attention to; retain, keep.

略

畝(亩)　mǔ
Unit of area.

略　lüè
Slightly; an outline, a sketch; leave out, omit; strategy, plan; seize, capture.

畢(毕)　bì
To complete, to terminate; entire, all.

異

異(异)　yì
Different; extraordinary, outstanding; surprised; other, foreign.

番　fān
A turn, a time.

畫(画)　huà
A drawing, a painting; draw, paint; a stroke of a Chinese character.

男

當(当)　dāng
To be, to act as; manage; withstand; during; ought.

男　nán
Male, man.

疆　jiāng
A limit, a boundary, frontier, border.

shí

rock

RADICAL 112

Properties of the rock – its hardness and unyielding substance, and at the same time its very brittleness – come through in examples of the 'rock' radical. Break (破), shatter (碎), collide (碰) are listed; so are grind (磨) and investigate (研). 研 probably carries the 'rock' radical because only something relatively impenetrable needs to undergo an investigation.

碰

碎 suì
Broken, fragmented, cracked.

礙(碍) ài
To obstruct, to impede, to block.

碰 pèng
To bump, to collide; to meet, to come across; to try, to probe.

碎

研

硬

碼(码) mǎ
A symbol or article for numerals; a yard.

碧 bì
Bluish-green; green jade.

碗 wǎn
A bowl.

研(研) yán
To grind; investigate, research.

確(确) què
True, real; firmly.

磨 mò
A grindstone; to grind.

硬 yìng
Hard, unyielding, firm; insistently; uneasy, unnatural.

磚(砖) zhuān
Brick, tile.

礫(砾) lì
Small stones; gravel.

礦(矿) kuàng
Minerals; a mine.

磊 lěi
Rocky.

shān

mountain

RADICAL 46

While some characters cannot be linked in a straight-forward way to their radical, the 'mountain' radical is truly an exception because almost every single character featured concerns hills, mounds, peaks, ridges, or of the steep and precipitous heights that characterise them.

峭 qiào
Precipitous, steep, abrupt; strict, stern.

峻 jùn
Lofty, high, steep; stern, severe.

峽(峡) xiá
A gorge, a sharp ravine; straits; isthmus.

嶺

島

嶄

峨 é
High, lofty, steep.

巒(峦) luán
Low hills; ridges.

巖(岩) yán
A precipice; a rock.

岳 yuè
A lofty mountain.

岸 àn
A bank, a shore; a
beach, a coast.

峯 fēng
A summit, a peak.

島(岛) dǎo
An island, an isle.

嶺(岭) lǐng
A peak; a ridge, a
mountain range.

岡(冈) gāng
The ridge of a hill.

崗(岗) gǎng
A mound; a post.

嶄(崭) zhǎn
High, lofty, prominent.

崩 bēng
To collapse; to fall into
ruin; to break down.

xué

cave

RADICAL 116

There are of course a fair number of characters directly related to cave, these being 窩 , 窠 , 窟 . Others relate to entering or looking out from within; and in the case of 窮 , by putting together the 'cave' radical plus individual characters for 'body' and 'bent', the idea of poverty is effectively conveyed.

穿

窺（窥） kuì
To peep, to pry.

窈 yǎo
Deep; profound.

窠 kē
A nest; a den.

窟 kū
A hole; a cave; a furrow.

究　jiū
Examine, investigate; after all, finally.

空　kōng
The sky; the air; heaven; empty; unreal.

穿　chuān
To bore through, to perforate, to pass through; to dress, to wear.

突　tū
Suddenly, abruptly; to protrude, to project; to break through; to offend; a chimney.

窄　zhǎi
Narrow; narrow-minded.

窗　chuāng
Window.

窝(窝)　wō
Den, nest, lair; hideout: shelter, hide; a hollow.

窮(穷)　qióng
Poor; exhausted; extreme.

fù

mound

RADICAL 170

阝

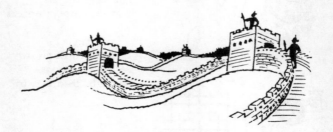

Radicals 170 and 163 look identical, but one elementary way of distinguishing between the two is that the 'mound' radical is located consistently on the left side of the character. The classic symbol of balance and symmetry, yīnyáng (陰陽), can be seen to take the 'mound' radical too.

防

防 fáng
Guard against, prevent; defence, protection; a dyke.

附 fù
Supplementary, additional; attach, adhere to; be near to.

降 jiàng
Drop, descend.

限 xiàn
Limit; to limit, to define.

陪 péi
To accompany.

陸(陆) lù
The shore; land, continent.

隆 lóng
Grand; solemn; prosperous, flourishing; a peal of thunder.

隊(队) duì
A line, a squad, the ranks; a company, a team.

隨(随) suí
Follow; as one pleases; at one's convenience.

險(险) xiǎn
Danger, risk; dangerous; nearly, almost.

際(际) jì
A border, limit.

隔 gé
Separate, cut off; apart.

邑

yì

city

RADICAL 163

阝

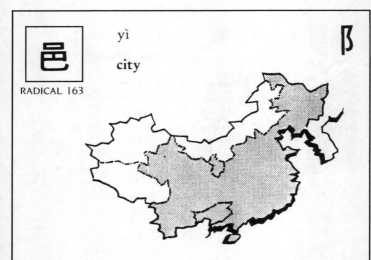

Generally, this radical means 'city' but from its usage it appears to mean 'district' or 'a division of any sort'. Divisions could encompass country or city, suburban areas or province and prefecture, even department. It is always found on the right portion of the character.

鄉(乡) xiāng
Village, countryside; home-town, native place.

都 dū
City, capital, a metropolis.

郎 láng
Young man; gentleman.

鄉

鄰（邻）lín
Neighbour, neighbourhood; near, next, neighbouring.

邦 bāng
A state, a country, a nation.

郊 jiāo
Suburban areas; country, outskirts.

郭 guō
Second wall of a city.

郵（邮）yóu
Pertaining to postal.

部 bù
A section, a part; a ministry, a department, a board.

都 dōu
All, altogether; already.

鄙 bǐ
Rustic; low, base, mean.

郡 jùn
An administrative district; a country (archaic).

THINGS

衣	宀	舟	匕
糸	冖	斤	酉
巾	瓦	干	皿
貝	广	戈	斗
門	网	弓	臼
戶	耒	刀	缶
片	車	矢	卩
		聿	

yī

clothing

RADICAL 145

Individual items of clothing and attire like gowns, jackets, trousers, skirts, socks and stockings all take the 'clothing' radical. Sleeves, though not worn separately, and lining, which should be invisible, are parts of clothing, and belong to the same radical family.

袖 xiù
Sleeve.

袍 páo
Robe, gown.

裁 cái
To cut, to trim; to reduce; decision, judgement.

裙 qún
Skirt.

補

補（补）bǔ
To repair, to patch; to make up; to nourish.

裝（装）zhuāng
To dress up; to pretend; to load; to install, fix.

製（制）zhì
To make, to create; to produce, to manufacture.

裙

褲（裤）kù
Trousers, pants.

襖（袄）ǎo
Coat, jacket.

襪（袜）wà
Socks; stockings.

褂 guà
Outer jacket, a coat.

裏（里）lǐ
Inside; lining.

裂 liè
Crack; tear; rip.

被 bèi
Quilt, blanket; to cover, to wear; by (indicating the passive voice).

裂

糸

silk

糸 (丝)

RADICAL 120

The 'silk' radical 糸, which resembles a skein of silk, is responsible for a whole host of characters. Among these are rope or string (繩), thread or wire (綫), web (網), and various characters meaning 'bind' or 'fasten'. Weave, knit, sew, and embroider – making fabric or items out of fibre or yarn – are other relevant examples.

紙 (纸) zhǐ
Paper.

綁 (绑) bǎng
Tie, bind, fasten together.

絲 (丝) sī
Silk.

綉 (绣) xiù
Embroider.

緊

緊（紧） jǐn
Tight; urgent.

綿（绵） mián
Floss silk; soft;
continuous.

網（网） wǎng
Net; web; network.

綫（线） xiàn
Thread; filament; wire.

縫（缝） féng
Sew, stitch; mend,
patch.

織（织） zhī
Knit; weave.

網

繞（绕） rào
Coil, entwine; revolve;
make a detour.

繫（系） xì
Tie up; fasten.

編

編（编） biān
Braid, to plait; to
weave, to knit; arrange;
edit, compile.

繼（继） jì
Continue, succeed,
follow after.

繭（茧） jiǎn
The cocoon of a
silkworm.

jīn

cloth

RADICAL 50

Flags, banners, tents, streamers, sails, curtains and screens – which generally require large expanses of cloth, issue from this radical. In ancient times, notices and announcements were written on scrolls, giving rise to the character 帖 . Smaller personal items like belt (带), handkerchief (帕) and hat (帽) are included as well.

帕

帕 pà
A turban; a handkerchief.

帷 wéi
Curtain.

幅 fú
The width of cloth; a roll (of paper); a scroll (of painting).

帳

布　bù
Cloth; arrange; publish, make known.

帆　fān
Sail, canvas.

帖　tiě
Invitation card; notice.

席　xí
Straw or bamboo mat; seat; banquet.

帽

帳（帐）zhàng
Tent; mosquito net; a scroll sent to mourners.

帽　mào
Hat, cap.

幕　mù
Tent; stage curtain or screen; movie screen; act of a play.

幕

幟（帜）zhì
A flag; a banner.

幡　fān
Streamers hung before a shrine.

幫（帮）bāng
To help; a group, a party.

貝 (贝)

bèi

money

RADICAL 154

Money, a most valuable asset, functions as a common radical. It features in characters like wealth (財), spending it (費), gambling it away (賭), earning it (賺), winning it (贏), a thief who steals it away (賊), buy and sell (買賣), expensive (貴), and the result of consumption – a bill (賬)!

販

財(财) cái
Property; wealth, valuables.

貨(货) huò
Goods, merchandise.

貪(贪) tān
Greedy, covetous.

販(贩) fàn
Buy and sell, trade; a peddler, a hawker.

費（费）fèi
Expenditure; spend, use, consume; waste.

貴（贵）guì
Expensive; honourable; noble.

資（资）zī
Wealth, property, capital; to give, to provide; aptitude; qualifications.

賊（贼）zéi
A thief, a burglar; a rebel, an enemy; undesirable person.

賞（赏）shǎng
Bestow, grant; reward; enjoy, appreciate.

賬（账）zhàng
Account, bill.

賜（赐）cì
Bestow, grant.

賭（赌）dǔ
Gamble, make a bet.

賺（赚）zhuàn
To earn, to gain, to make (money).

贏（赢）yíng
Win; score.

貴

$1/- $2/-

賊

贏

（门）

mén

door

RADICAL 169

Being an entrance as well as a frame constructed to impede entry, the door operates as the radical in such characters as open (開) and close (關, 閉, 圖). There are other ways of opening up – disclosure (闢) and penetration (闡). And as for forced entry the character shows, amusingly, a horse in the doorway (闖).

閃（闪）shǎn
A flash of light; avoid; sparkle.

闢（辟）pì
To open up; to refute.

闔（阖）hé
All, whole; shut, close.

闖（闯）chuǎng
To force one's way, to rush, to break through.

閑

閉（闭） bì
To shut; to obstruct.

閑（闲） xián
Unoccupied, free.

開（开） kāi
To open, to start.

關（关） guān
Close, shut; a frontier
gate, a pass; customs
station; a turning point;
involve.

閨（闺） guī
A small door; a
boudoir.

閉

闌（阑） lán
Railing; block; nearly
finished or completed.

閎（闳） hóng
Great, large.

開

閣（阁） gé
A chamber; a pavilion;
the cabinet.

闕（阙） què
The gate tower of an
imperial palace.

闡（阐） chǎn
To express; to disclose;
to enlighten.

hù

door

RADICAL 63

This radical also means 'door', but shows only one side of the door. It has fewer examples, although they are relevant ones. 所 is the general character for place, including offices and departments like clinic (診療所), research department (研究所), community centre (聯絡所), etc. 房 is of course house or room.

扇

扇 shān
To fan; stir, agitate.

所 suǒ
A place; an office, a centre.

房 fáng
House or apartment; room, chamber.

扁 biǎn
Flat.

片

piàn

slice

RADICAL 91

Make no mistake, too many pieces of paper can baffle the sense. Similarly, not taking the trouble to read signs properly could prove a pain in the behind. 片 is the radical meaning 'slice' or 'piece'. Most of the handful of characters with this radical are given below.

牌

版 bǎn
A register; a block for printing; an edition; a newspaper page.

牌 pái
Board; tablet or card (for advertisements, signs, notices, etc.).

牘(牍) dú
A note, a letter, a document.

roof

RADICAL 40

Everything under one roof – with a domestic animal like the pig one gets a home (家), with a woman one keeps the peace (安), with prized possessions like porcelain, money and jade there is treasure (寶). The roof provides shelter, and lodging (室) is therefore arrival (至) under a roof (宀).

家

宮 gōng
The palace; an ancestral temple.

家 jiā
A household, a family; a school (of learning); a specialist.

密 mì
Close together, dense; closely related, intimate; secret; precise.

富 fù
Wealthy; abundant.

寒 hán
Cold, chilly; poor,
needy.

寡 guǎ
Few, scant; a widow.

寶（宝） bǎo
Treasure; precious,
valuable; highly prized.

寶

宿 sù
Lodging; long-standing.

守 shǒu
To guard, to defend; to
abide by; wait.

安 ān
Calm, quiet; safe; to
pacify; to install.

守

定 dìng
Tranquil, stable, fixed;
to determine, to decide;
firm; order, arrange;
surely, certainly.

客 kè
Guest, visitor;
passenger, customer.

室 shì
House, room; office;
restaurant.

安

cover

RADICAL 8

Though the 'cover' radical resembles the 'roof' radical somewhat, it looks more like a lid, without the two eaves which protrude from the edges of the 'roof'. There is no apparent connection between the radical and its character examples, except perhaps in pavilion or shelter (亭) and capital (京).

亭

交 jiāo
Deliver, hand over; acquaint, befriend; intersect.

亭 tíng
A pavilion; a kiosk, a shelter.

亮 liàng
Bright, clear; elucidate; loud and clear.

wǎ

tile

RADICAL 98

Earthenware and crockery like jars, vases and urns, and bottles, pitchers and jugs can be seen to bear the same radical. More precious and fragile porcelain and chinaware belong here too.

瓶 píng
Bottle, jar, pitcher, jug, vase.

瓷 cí
Porcelain.

甄 zhēn
Examine; distinguish.

甕(瓮) wèng
Urn; earthen jar.

广

lean-to

RADICAL 53

Another shelter radical, this one is like a roof seen from the side. Here, the examples do relate to particular places like the verandah (廊), living room area (廳), block of apartments or mansion (厦), factory (廠), kitchen (厨), etc. However, the dot has been removed in some simplifications.

底

底　dǐ
Bottom, base; below; the end; a draft; reach.

店　diàn
A shop, a store; an inn, a tavern.

座　zuò
Seat; measure word for mountain, bridge, tall building, reservoir, etc.

厨

庭

廈

厦 shà
A tall building; mansion.

廊 láng
Porch; corridor; verandah.

厨 chú
A kitchen.

廳（厅） tīng
A living room; a parlour; a dining room.

厠（厕） cè
A toilet, a lavatory.

廢（废） fèi
Cancel, discontinue; spoilt, worthless, waste.

庭 tíng
A courtyard; a court of justice.

廂 xiāng
A side-room; a suburb; a compartment.

廣（广） guǎng
Wide, extensive, broad, spacious; common, popular; expand, spread.

廠（厂） chǎng
A factory; a plant; a workhouse.

网 net

RADICAL 122

罒　罓

Evil deeds and wrongdoing will have their just deserts.
Punishment (罰), for instance, is inflicted upon the
criminal or offender, and for his wrong deed (非), the
evildoer is trapped in his guilt and suffering.

罪

罔　wǎng
Deceive; nothing.

罪　zuì
A crime, offence; guilt;
suffering.

罰(罚)　fá
Punish, fine, forfeit.

置　zhì
To place, to put;
arrange, install; buy.

lěi

plough

RADICAL 127

The work of ploughing the fields for cultivation of crops (耕), weeding (耘), and implements needed to facilitate such a labour like the rake or harrow (耙) are obviously linked. Their common denominator is the 'plough' radical, which supplies the meaning to all these characters.

耗　hào
Waste time, squander; consume; bad news, information.

耘　yún
To weed.

耙(耙)　bà
A rake; a harrow.

耕　gēng
Plough, cultivate.

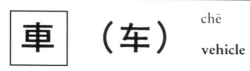

車 （车）

chē

vehicle

RADICAL 159

Under the 'car' or 'vehicle' radical are various characters for carriage like 輦, 軫 and 轎; also, parts of the wheel, which keep the vehicle in motion. Its appearance in characters like transport or carry (載) makes the meaning even more apparent. Perhaps the most graphic example is the character for rumble or explode (轟), where three cars are involved in a pile-up!

轟

轟（轰）hōng
Bang, crash, roar (of thunder or any explosive noise); bombard.

軍（军）jūn
An army; troops; soldiers; corps.

輕（轻）qīng
Light; minor; pay scant attention to; hasty.

輪

輛（辆） liàng
A measure word for vehicles.

輪（轮） lún
A wheel; a gear.

輻（辐） fú
Spokes of a wheel.

輸（输） shū
Transport, convey; lose, be defeated.

轆

轆（辘） lù
A pulley; wheel and axle; a windlass; the rumbling of carriages.

輳（辏） còu
The hub of a wheel.

轄（辖） xiá
The linchpin of a wheel; govern, control.

載

輾（辗） zhǎn
To roll; turn over.

轉（转） zhuǎn
To revolve; to rotate, to turn, to change; to transfer.

載（载） zài
To load, to carry, to transport; to fill with.

zhōu

boat

RADICAL 137

The 'boat' radical is positioned consistently on the left side of the character, and is always a direct clue to the meaning. Here can be found seaworthy vessels of various shapes and sizes, from the formidable warship down to the modest sampan. About the only odd one out is 般 , having no connection to boats, ships, or the sea.

航

航 háng
A boat; a large vessel; sail; fly (a plane).

舰(舰) jiàn
Warship; naval vessel; man-of-war.

舵 duò
Rudder; helm.

船

艇

舷

船　chuán
A boat, a ship; any floating vessel.

艘　sōu
Numeral for ships and vessels.

舳　zhú
Stern of a ship.

艙（舱）cāng
The hold of a ship or an aeroplane.

艇　tǐng
A light boat; a canoe; a punt, a barge.

舶　bó
Oceangoing ship.

舢板　shānbǎn
Sampan.

舷　xián
The side of a ship; the bulwarks; the gunwale.

舫　fǎng
A boat, a vessel.

般　bān
Sort, kind, class, manner.

jīn

axe

RADICAL 69

Although the meaning of this character is 'a unit of weight', the radical is derived from the character 斧 or axe. It is therefore no accident that 'to chop off' or 'to cut in two' (斬) and 'to cut' or 'to break off' (斷) have this particular radical.

斬

斧 fǔ
An axe, a hatchet.

斬(斩) zhǎn
To chop off, to cut in two.

斷(断) duàn
Cut off, break off; discontinue.

gān

shield

干 was the ancient character for 'shield'. Unfortunately, no connection can be drawn based on the mere handful of examples. The only exception to this is 幹, which means 'do' or 'manage', or 'skilful' or 'able'. Incidentally, its simplified character is none other than 干.

幹

平 píng
Flat, smooth; fair;
peaceful; ordinary.

幸 xìng
Fortunate.

并 bìng
Combine; and.

幹(干) gàn
Trunk; make, manage;
skilful, able.

戈

gē

lance

RADICAL 62

Ancient warriors never advanced into battle without being armed with the necessary weaponry, hence this 'lance' radical accounts for characters like 戎 (military), 戰 (war), 戡 (suppress), 截 (intercept), 戳 (pierce), and 戮 (slaughter).

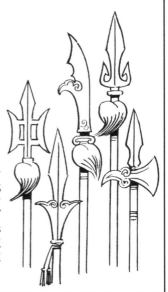

戰

戎 róng
Military; army.

戰(战) zhàn
War, battle; to fight; to tremble, to quiver.

戒 jiè
Take precaution, guard against; give up (a habit).

戡 chéng
To finish, to
accomplish; to become;
to win, to succeed.

戡 kān
Suppress or subdue; to
put down.

戚 qī
Relative; sorrow.

截 jié
Cut; intercept, stop.

戍 shù
Guard, defend.

戲(戏) xì
Play; game; make fun of;
theatrical performance,
drama, play.

戴 dài
Wear, bear; respect,
support.

戳 chuō
To poke, to pierce;
stamp, seal.

戮 lù
Kill, stab, slaughter, put
to death.

gōng

bow

RADICAL 57

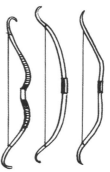

In archery, the string of the bow has to be stretched as far back as possible to release the arrow. This explains therefore the presence of the 'bow' radical in characters like 張 (expand, stretch), 弘 (expand, enlarge), 引 (stretch), and 彎 (bend). Shooting a catapult requires a similar skill, hence 彈 .

引

引 yǐn
Draw (a bow); stretch; guide, lead; to refer to.

弘 hóng
Great, expanded; to expand, to enlarge.

弭 mǐ
To stop; to check.

弦

弦　xián
The elastic cord on a bow; musical chord; a crescent moon.

弩　nǔ
A crossbow.

弱　ruò
Weak, feeble.

彈

彈（弹）　tán
To flick, to flip; to shoot, to snap; to spring, to bounce.

張（张）　zhāng
To open up; to stretch; to expand, to look; a measure word for leaf, sheet, piece, etc.

強　qiáng
Strong and healthy; forcefully; firm.

彎

彌（弥）　mí
Full, whole; to make up, to amend.

彎（弯）　wān
Draw a bow; bent, curved, arched; bend, turn.

dāo

knife

刂

RADICAL 18

More often than not, the 'knife' radical appears in its variant form on the character's right side. The sharpness of the knife blade (利) is useful not only in cutting, chopping, dividing; frequent references to sharp tongues have proven that knives are not the only instruments with potent cutting edges!

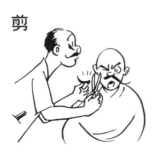

剛(刚) gāng
Solid, hard, firm, unyielding; just, recently.

剪 jiǎn
Shears, scissors; cut, chop, shear.

割 gē
Cut, sever, divide.

切 qiē
Cut, chop.

利

分 fēn
Divide, separate; distribute, distinguish; portion, part.

利 lì
Sharp, acute; advantageous, useful; smooth-going.

劃（划） huà
Draw, classify, divide; plan, planning.

刻

刻 kè
To carve, to engrave; harsh.

劍（剑） jiàn
A sword, a dagger.

初 chū
At first; beginning.

判 pàn
Divide, differentiate; judge, decide.

別 biě
Leave, depart; classify, distinguish; another; do not.

刺

刺 cì
A thorn, a sting, a prick; to pierce, to thrust, to stab.

shǐ

arrow

RADICAL 111

Unlike the 'bow' radical, the 'arrow' radical's examples are scant. Two of the more common examples happen to be 短 (short, referring to something inanimate), and 矮 (short, this time in reference to a person). Neither is related to the arrow in any way.

矮

知 zhī
Know, perceive, be aware.

矩 jǔ
A rule, a law, a pattern.

短 duǎn
Short; lacking.

矮 ǎi
Short; low in rank or position.

匕　**ladle**

RADICAL 21

Another radical which works in mysterious ways, it has given rise to characters of widely different meanings. Transform or alter (化), north (北), and spoon (匙) come arbitrarily under the same radical, though only spoon bears any relation to the radical.

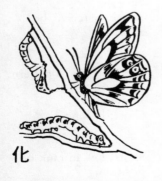

化 huà
Change, alter, transform; dissolve, melt.

北 běi
North.

匙 chí
A spoon.

酉 wine

RADICAL 164

Wine is a necessary ingredient at social gatherings. Thus, when one entertains or attends a social function, one is said to 'pledge with wine' (應酬). Vinegar (醋) is made from beer or weak wine, and the Chinese expression of 'eating vinegar' connotes jealousy. The 'wine' radical is also prominent in characters for 'drunken' and 'sober' states.

吃醋

酸 suān
Sour; grieved, sad; ache due to overfatigue or illness.

酬 chóu
To pledge with wine, to entertain; to repay, to reward.

醋 cù
Vinegar; jealousy.

酣 hān
Merry from drinking;
rapturous.

酒 jiǔ
Liquor, wine, spirit.

配 pèi
To matchmake; to
blend, to compose;
worth, fit.

醉 zuì
To be drunk.

酷 kù
Cruel, harsh,
oppressive; very,
extremely.

酤 gū
Wine; buy or sell wine.

醜（丑） chǒu
Ugly; disgraceful,
shameful.

醬（酱） jiàng
Soy sauce; gravy.

醒 xǐng
Awake, sober; awaken,
come to realize.

酥 sū
Crispy; soft, tender;
butter, cheese.

mǐn

vessel

RADICAL 108

A vessel or receptacle of some sort, this radical invariably appears at the bottom of the character. The types of receptacle vary from basins and tubs to plates, dishes and trays, even boxes. As for 盛, which means 'luxuriant', 'flourishing', the combination of 成 and 皿 no doubt suggests that one's plate is filled abundantly.

盆 pén
A basin; a pot; a tub.

盈 yíng
Be full of, be filled with; a surplus of.

盏(盞) zhǎn
Small cup; measure word for lamp or cup.

盒 hé
Box, casket, carton.

盛

盛 shèng
Luxuriant, prosperous, flourishing; strong, grand, splendid; widely, to a great extent.

盎 àng
An ancient vessel with a big belly and a small mouth.

盡(尽) jìn
Completed, finished; the utmost, the last; fulfil.

盤

盤(盘) pán
A plate, a dish, a tray; to circle around; in detail; expenses.

監(监) jiān
Examine carefully, supervise; a prison, a jail.

盥 guàn
Wash (the hands or face).

盒

益 yì
Benefit, profit, advantage; increase.

盂 yú
A broad-mouthed receptacle for holding liquid.

斗 dǒu

scoop

RADICAL 68

Seeing that this radical means 'a peck measure' or 'scoop', referring therefore to the measurement of grain, it is present in the following handful of examples. In fact, the radical is itself a pictograph of a scoop – with the stroke sloping downwards, and the two dots resembling two grains.

斜

料 liào
Raw materials; grain; suppose, guess.

斜 xié
Slanting, inclining; sloping; oblique.

斟 zhēn
To pour out.

jiù

mortar

臾

RADICAL 134

A variant form of the 'mortar' radical manifests itself in 擧 (raise, hold up), and similarly in 與 (and, with; give; help; intimate) and 興 (launch, establish; interest).

擧

舀 yǎo
To bale out water; to dip.

舊(旧) jiù
Old, ancient; worn, second-hand.

擧(举) jǔ
Raise, lift, hold up; praise; behaviour; begin, inaugurate; cite.

缶 fǒu

earthenware

RADICAL 121

Earthen vessels and jars carry the 'earthenware' radical, and it is interesting to find that characters meaning 'deficient', 'lacking', 'having a shortcoming', like 缺 and 罅 have the same radical too. The original meaning of 缺 is 'broken' and 罅 is 'crack' or 'rift'.

罐

缸 gāng
Earthen vessel; jar.

罐 guàn
Can; pot; tin.

缺 quē
Lack; incomplete; a vacancy; absent.

罌（甖） yīng
Jar; vase.

seal

RADICAL 26

In shape, the 'seal' radical is evolved from the ancient seal script of a kneeling figure. Among the characters with this radical are 印 (seal, stamp), and 卷 (book, volume). In addition, 危 (perilous, dangerous, critical) is another example.

印 yìn
A seal, a rubber-stamp; trace; print; tally with.

卸 xiè
Unload; dismantle; get rid of.

卷 juàn
A book, a volume; test paper; a volume (measure word).

yù

brush

RADICAL 129

Calligraphy is an art requiring much discipline and control, so with this radical – derived from the action of a hand holding up a writing brush firmly – we get characters meaning 'study' (肄) and 'solemn' or 'serious' (肅).

肅

肄 yì
Study.

肆 sì
Reckless, unrestrained.

肅(肃) sù
Respectful, solemn;
stern, majestic, serious.

肇 zhào
To occur, to cause.

ACTIONS

見 日 彳 口
欠 立 走 止
食 工 行 示
言 疋 殳 攴

勹

見　（见）

jiàn

see

RADICAL 147

Looking at, viewing, examining, inspecting – are possible because of the faculty of vision. Thus characters representing these acts of seeing carry the 'to see' radical. One most fascinating example is 'covet' (覬), which means, literally, 'to cast one's greedy eyes on'. And 展覽會 is an exhibition, a display meant for public viewing.

觀

規（规） guī
Law, rule, regulation; plan; advise, warn.

視（视） shì
Regard, consider; see, look; inspect, examine.

覥 tiǎn
Shy, timid.

親

覩（觇） dǔ
To see.

親（亲） qīn
Parents; related by
blood or marriage;
personal; close, dear,
intimate; to kiss.

覬（觊） jì
Covet.

覺

覯（觏） gòu
See, meet.

觀（观） guān
Look at, view, inspect; a
view, a sight; an opinion
or viewpoint.

覺（觉） jiào
Sleep, nap.

覺（觉） jué
Sense; feel, perceive; be
aware of, understand,
realize.

覽（览） lǎn
See, sightsee, view; read.

覽

qiàn

to yawn

RADICAL 76

Meaning 'to yawn', the original seal character shows a person yawning with mouth wide open. As the mouth is involved in laughing and crying and singing, this radical occurs in characters like 欣 (glad), 歡 (pleased), 歌 (song), and 欷 (sigh).

歡

歔 xū
Sob in secret.

欷 xī
Sob; sigh.

歡（欢）huān
Jolly, cheerful, pleased.

欺

次 cì
Order, position; inferior; a time (measure word); a place.

欺 qī
Cheat, deceive, fool; bully, insult, abuse.

歉

欣 xīn
Happy, glad, delighted.

欲 yù
Desire, wish, hope; need; about to, going to (happen).

款 kuǎn
Sincere; entertain; sum of money, fund.

歌

歇 xiē
Rest; stop.

歉 qiàn
Bad harvest; sorry, regretful.

歌 gē
Song, ballad; to sing.

食

shí

food

RADICAL 184

食 (饣)

People eat for basic survival as well as for pleasure, and as a radical, it is common to many characters. Being full (飽) and hungry (餓), nourish (養), meal (餐), are significant examples. Individual types of food also carry the 'food' radical, these being the staple of rice (飯), biscuit or cake (餅), dumpling (餃) and bun (饅).

飽

養（养） yǎng
To raise, bring up; to support; to rear; convalesce, nourish; cultivate.

飽（饱） bǎo
To be full, satiated.

飯（饭） fàn
Cooked rice; a meal.

餅

飲（饮） yǐn
Drink.

餅（饼） bǐng
Cake, pastry, biscuit.

餐 cān
A meal.

餓（饿） è
Hungry, starved.

餓

饑（饥） jī
Hungry, insufficient;
famine.

館（馆） guǎn
A hotel, a restaurant; a
hall; a commercial
service centre.

饅（馒） mán
Steamed bread or bun.

餞（饯） jiàn
Give a farewell party.

餘

餘（余） yú
Remainder, surplus;
beyond, after.

饒（饶） ráo
Abundant, plentiful,
resourceful; to spare, to
forgive.

yán

speech

言 (讠)

RADICAL 149

Although the faculty of speech can be used to advantage – to thank, to educate, to caution, to invite, etc., abuse leads to idle talk, lying, swearing, boasting, and other undesirable acts. The very common 'speech' radical mostly occurs on the left side; whenever it appears at the bottom, it is not simplified.

討論

討論(讨论) tǎolùn
To discuss; to talk over.

訪(访) fǎng
Call upon, visit; enquire into, search for.

誓 shì
Swear, vow, make an oath.

詩(诗) shī
Poetry, poem, verse.

誇（夸）　kuā
Praise, extol; boast, brag.

請（请）　qǐng
Request, ask for; invite; a courteous word meaning 'please'.

誦（诵）　sòng
Recite, read out loud; praise.

謊（谎）　huǎng
Lie, falsehood.

講（讲）　jiǎng
Talk, converse; explain.

謝（谢）　xiè
Express gratitude, thank; apologise; decline, reject; wither, fade.

談（谈）　tán
To speak, to converse; gossip, chat.

謠（谣）　yáo
Folk song, ballad, rhymes; rumour.

警　jǐng
Notify, caution, warn; police; an emergency.

yuē

to say

RADICAL 73

The radical 'to say' is truly more of a mystery. There is remarkably little to say about it, except for 'verses' (曲) and 'meeting' or 'assembly' (會), which does require verbal participation.

曲

曲　qǔ
Song, lyrics; classical Chinese verses.

更　gēng
Alter, change; night watch.

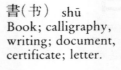

書（书） shū
Book; calligraphy, writing; document, certificate; letter.

曼 màn
Graceful, fine, handsome; long, prolonged.

曹 cáo
A company, a class, a generation.

替 tì
To substitute, to replace; on behalf of.

曾 céng
Already; at some time in the past.

最 zuì
Most, best, to the highest degree.

曳 yè
Drag, haul, tug, tow.

會（会） huì
Assemble, meet together; association, society; able to.

lì

stand

RADICAL 117

A person standing with both arms raised and legs astride is the way the character was originally represented in its seal form. 'To stand' (站) is therefore directly related to the radical, and in 'compete' or 'contend' (競), there are two males (兄) standing side by side in competition.

站 zhàn
To stand; station or stop (as in railway station or bus stop).

競 (竞) jìng
Compete, contend, strive.

端 duān
Proper, decent, direct; to carry.

gōng

work

RADICAL 48

To say the least, the following examples show a set of vastly different characters all nevertheless belonging to the same radical family of 'work'. Perhaps 'witchcraft' (巫) is similar to being 'ingenious' and 'cunning' (巧) in that both require a special craft or skill.

巧

巧 qiǎo
Skilful, ingenious, clever; cunning, deceitful; coincidentally.

巨 jù
Huge, tremendous, gigantic.

巫 wū
Shaman, witch, wizard.

halt

RADICAL 162

This radical is only seen in its variant form. The idea of journeying forth and a passage is present in most of the character examples, even if sometimes it is in pursuit (追), to escape from (逃), or being lost (迷). Meeting, greeting and arriving and concepts of distance like far (遠) and near (近) have the same radical too.

遲

過（过）guò
Cross, pass; across, over; spend time; after; exceed; fault, mistake.

道 dào
Road, path; channel; way, method.

達（达）dá
Extend; reach; understand thoroughly; express, communicate.

追

追　zhuī
Chase, pursue; trace, get to the bottom of; seek; recall.

逃　táo
Escape, run away from; evade, shirk.

途　tú
Way, road, route.

遇　yù
Meet; receive; chance, opportunity.

迎

迎　yíng
Greet, welcome; move towards, meet head-on.

進(进)　jìn
Advance, move forward; enter; receive.

遲(迟)　chí
Slow, tardy.

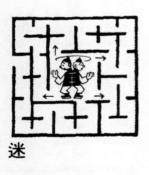

迷　mí
Be confused; be lost; be fascinated by; fan of, enthusiast of.

遠(远)　yuǎn
Far, distant, remote.

迷

近　jìn
Close, near.

chì

step

RADICAL 60

A radical with less examples to its credit than 辶 , it has nonetheless some characters of significance like 循 and 從 (follow), 往 (head towards), 還 (come back), and 徘徊 (pace), as anxious fathers are wont to do in ward corridors!

徒

徹(彻) chè
Thorough, penetrating.

徐 xú
Slowly, gently.

徒 tú
On foot; empty, bare; merely, only; in vain; apprentice, disciple.

循 xún
Follow, abide by.

徘徊

征 zhēng
Go on a journey, or an expedition; be drafted; collect, levy (taxes); ask for, solicit; sign, evidence.

律 lù
Law, statute, rule; restrain.

徘徊 páihuí
Pace up and down; hesitate, waver.

後

後(后) hòu
Behind, back; after, later.

復(复) fù
Turn around; answer; recover, resume; revenge; again.

德 dé
Virtue, morals; heart, mind; kindness, favour.

徑

徑(径) jìng
Footpath, path, track; way, means; directly, diameter.

御 yù
Drive (a carriage); imperial; resist, keep out, ward off.

走 zǒu

walk

走

RADICAL 156

Walking can be anything from a leisurely stroll to a brisk trot, or a walk almost like a run as in big walk contests. As such, the 'walk' radical includes the characters for 'overtake' (超) and 'hasten' (趕). Getting up from one's prostrate position on the bed (起) also means that one has to start walking about and administer the day's affairs.

趨(趋) qū
Hasten, hurry along; tend towards, tend to become.

趣 qù
Interest, delight; interesting.

赴 fù
Go to, attend.

超 chāo
Exceed, surpass, overtake; ultra-, super-, extra-; transcend, go beyond.

趟 tàng
A measure word (e.g. one trip).

赳 jiū
Valiant, gallant.

起 qǐ
Take up; set out, get up.

趁 chèn
Take advantage of; while, take the opportunity to (do something).

越 yuè
Get over, jump over; exceed, overstep; loud and strong, at a high pitch (describing voice or emotion).

趕(赶) gǎn
Catch up with, overtake; make a dash for; hurry through; drive away.

xíng

go

RADICAL 144

The 'go' radical is similar to the 'step' radical in appearance, except for the addition of the component on the right hand side. The radical 行 is stretched, and the middle element, which always varies, will then produce a different character.

衛

街 jiē
Street.

衝(冲) chōng
Hastily, hurriedly.

衛(卫) wèi
Defend, guard, protect.

殳

kill

RADICAL 79

Some of the common examples listed under this radical happen to be actions of violence, such as wrecking, damaging, beating, hitting, and killing. In fact, the seal form is of a hand holding a stick or club.

毀 huǐ
Destroy, ruin, damage; defame, slander.

毅 yì
Firm, resolute.

毆（殴） ōu
Beat up, hit.

殺（杀） shā
Kill, slaughter; fight.

RADICAL 31

enclosure

There is no question as to the meaning of this radical, and its relationship to its characters. Anything with a boundary of some sort is included. For a country, this would be the territorial borders, a drawing usually has a frame, a garden will have its hedges, fences or walls, and a prison its four depressing grey walls!

圍

困 kùn
Be stranded, be hard pressed; surround, pin down; tired; sleepy.

回 huí
Circle, winding; return, turn around; chapter.

圍(围) wéi
Enclose, surround; around.

圈　quān
Ring, ring-shaped
articles; sphere, scope,
circle; encircle, surround;
to mark with a circle.

固　gù
Solid, firm; resolutely;
consolidate; originally,
in the first place; no
doubt.

國（国）　guó
Country, state, nation;
of the state, national.

園（园）　yuán
Garden, area of land for
growing plants.

圓（圆）　yuán
Round, circular,
spherical; tactful,
satisfactory; justify.

圖（图）　tú
Picture, drawing; chart,
map; scheme, plan;
pursue, seek; intention.

團（团）　tuán
Round, circular; shaped
like a ball; roll; invite;
group, society,
organization; regiment;
a measure word.

zhǐ

to stop

RADICAL 77

Under this particular radical, there are two completely opposed characters: 正 (straight, upright, pure), and 歪 (crooked, devious). The fascinating feature of 歪 is in its combination of the two characters 不 (not) and 正 (straight) – literally, crooked is not straight!

正

歧　qí
Fork, branch; divergent, different.

正　zhèng
Straight, upright; in the middle; punctual; honest, upright; pure; principal, chief; regular; positive; exactly.

步

此 cǐ
This place, here; this kind, such as these.

步 bù
Step, pace; step; condition; walk; tread.

歲（岁） suì
Year; age.

武

歷（历） lì
Undergo, experience; one by one; calendar.

武 wǔ
Military; connected wtih boxing skill, swordplay, martial arts; chivalrous, valiant, fierce.

歪

歸（归） guī
Return, go back to, give back to; come together; turn over to.

歪 wāi
Crooked, slanting; devious, underhand.

示

shì

sign

RADICAL 113

礻

The manifestation of this radical in a character at once indicates that its meaning will be based on something of a divine nature, or pertaining to the spiritual – whether this be benign or evil. Meditation and worship, blessings like good fortune (福) and status (祿) bear this radical. However, 鬼 couples with 祟 in an oft-heard idiom 鬼鬼祟祟 (stealthy, furtive).

礼

禍（祸）huò
Misfortune, disaster; bring disaster upon, ruin.

禮（礼）lǐ
Ceremony, rite; courtesy, manners, etiquette; gift, present.

祥 xiáng
Auspicious, propitious, lucky.

祈禱

祈禱（祈祷） qídǎo
Pray, ask earnestly,
entreat.

禪（禅） chán
Deep meditation.

祠 cí
Ancestral temple.

福 fú
Good fortune, blessing,
happiness.

福

祿 lù
Salary, official pay.

社 shè
Organized body,
society, agency.

祖 zǔ
Grandfather; ancestor;
founder of a craft,
religious sect, school of
thought, etc.

祿

祝 zhù
Express good wishes.

神 shén
Supernatural, magical;
God, deity; spirit,
mind; expression.

祟 suì
Evil spirit, ghost.

RADICAL 66

knock

攵

The hand is engaged in the activity of knocking or hitting, or, as the case may be, rescuing (救), releasing (放), changing (改), receiving (收), scattering (散) and teaching (教). In the other characters, many denote actions of attacking, fighting, beating.

數

改 gǎi
Change, transfer; alter, revise; rectify; switch over to.

教 jiāo
Teach, instruct.

敵 (敌) dí
Enemy, foe; fight.

數 (数) shù
Number, figure.

放

放 fàng
Let go, release; let off; expand; blossom, open, put in, add to; put, place; send away; show.

政 zhèng
Politics; administrative aspects of government.

攻 gōng
Attack; accuse; study, specialize in.

散

救 jiù
Save; help.

败(敗) bài
Defeat, fail; counteract; decay, wither.

敢 gǎn
Bold, courageous; dare, have the confidence to.

敲

散 sǎn
Come loose, fall apart; scattered.

敬 jìng
Respect; offer politely and respectfully.

敲 qiāo
Knock, beat; fleece, overcharge.

wrap

RADICAL 20

The action of wrapping also connotes embracing or enveloping of something. What is shown in the seal character appears to be a person bent over and with arms curved. The body is curved and bundled up in the state of creeping and crawling (匍匐). To gang up with (勾) has the 'wrap' or 'envelop' radical containing a hook.

包

匍匐 púfú
Crawl, creep; lie
prostrate.

勾 gōu
Cancel, cross out; draw;
induce, gang up with.

包 bāo
Wrap; bundle, package;
protuberance; include,
contain; guarantee; hire.

CHARACTERISTICS

辛	力
白	广
黑	幺
大	老
方	歹

xīn

bitter

RADICAL 160

In the main, the most common examples show the radical on both sides. For instance, 'manage' has 力 or 'strength' squeezed in the middle (辦); 'differentiate' has ⺉ or a curved 'knife' in the centre (辨); 'argue' naturally has 言, 'speech' in its midst (辯); and 'braid' has the insertion of 糸, 'silk' (辮).

辮

辭(辞) cí
Diction; a type of classical Chinese literature; take leave; decline; dismiss; shirk.

辮(辫) biàn
Plait, braid; pigtail.

辣 là
Spicy, peppery, hot; stinging (of smell or taste); vicious, ruthless.

辜 gū
Guilt, crime.

辟 bì
Monarch, sovereign; ward off, keep away.

辟 pì
Open up (territory, land), break (ground); penetrating, incisive; refute, repudiate.

辦(办) bàn
Do, manage, attend to; set up, prepare; punish (legally), administer justice.

辨 biàn
Differentiate, distinguish, discriminate.

辯(辩) biàn
Argue, dispute, debate.

bái

white

RADICAL 106

White is equivalent to purity. Therefore, the emperor or sovereign, traditionally regarded as invested with supreme authority, is expected to have an unblemished record. The character for 'emperor' is written with the 'white' radical.

皎 jiǎo
Clear and bright.

皓 hào
White; bright, luminous.

魄 pò
Soul; vigour, spirit.

皇 huáng
Emperor, sovereign.

hēi

black

RADICAL 203

Just as white stands for purity and brightness, black represents darkness, gloom and defilement, certainly less positive attributes. Bring together 'black' (黑) and 'out' (出), and the result is the character for dismissal (黜).

默 mò
Silent, tacit; write from memory.

黛 dài
A black pigment used by women in ancient times to paint their eyebrows.

黜 chù
Remove somebody from office, dismiss.

大 dà

big

RADICAL 37

A man with hands outstretched – which has evolved into the character for 'big'. In 'sky' or 'heaven', an additional horizontal stroke is added on top of the man, suggesting a higher authority. However, in a few of the characters where the 'big' radical is placed above, the meanings are those of mastery or power.

天 tiān
Sky; day; weather; nature; God; Heaven.

失 shī
Lose; miss; mistake; break (a promise).

套 tào
Sheath, cover; cover with; overlap; harness; knot; copy; formula.

奇 qí
Strange, rare, unusual;
surprise, wonder.

奔 bēn
Run quickly; hurry,
hasten, rush; flee.

奏 zòu
Play (music), perform
(on a musical
instrument); achieve,
produce.

奕 yì
Radiating power and
vitality.

奪（夺） duó
Take by force, seize;
compete, contend for;
deprive.

奘 zhuǎng
Big and thick, stout,
robust.

獎（奖） jiǎng
Encourage, praise,
reward.

奮（奋） fèn
Exert oneself, act
vigorously; raise, lift.

fāng

square

RADICAL 70

Also a derivative of 'man' (人) and 'big' (大), 方 is like a man whose shoulders are squared, hence the meaning. This is again, however, one of those radicals which do not actively contribute to meaning, which should be apparent from the examples listed.

旁

施 shī
Execute, carry out; bestow, grant; impose; apply.

旁 páng
Side; other, else.

旌 jīng
Ancient banner.

旅 lǚ
Travel; brigade; troops.

旖旎 yǐnǐ
Charming and gentle.

族 zú
Clan; race or
nationality; class or
group.

於 yú
Towards, out of, up to.

旗 qí
Flag, banner.

旋 xuán
Revolve, circle; return;
soon.

力

lì

strength

RADICAL 19

Signs of industry and exertion mark the 'strength' radical. The character for 'move' attaches 'heavy' (重) on the left to the radical (力) on the right – applying energy to a heavy object. Similarly, 'encourage' (勉) and (勸) need strength, and definitely 'success' (勝) also derives from having put in strength and energy.

勁(劲) jìng
Strong, powerful, sturdy.

勇 yǒng
Brave, courageous.

勉 miǎn
Exert, strive; encourage.

動(动) dòng
Move; act; change; touch; arouse (emotion).

動

務（务） wù
Affair, business; be engaged in doing.

勝（胜） shèng
Victory, success; surpass; wonderful; be equal to.

勞（劳） láo
Work, labour; fatigue; meritorious deed, service.

勞

勢（势） shì
Power, force; circumstances, situation; sign, gesture.

勤 qín
Industrious, hard-working; frequently, regularly.

勸（劝） quàn
Advise, urge, persuade; encourage.

助

努 nǔ
Exert, put in (strength).

助 zhù
Help, assist, aid.

功 gōng
Merit, achievement; skill; work.

疒

disease

RADICAL 104

At one glance, 疒 is a radical which unmistakably signifies disease. Starting from the blanket character for a sick condition (病), one soon finds that it forms the root of every imaginable affliction – insanity, emaciation, malaria (瘧), smallpox, paralysis (癱), cancer (癌), to name but a few.

癢

病　bìng
Sick, ill; disease; fault, defect.

症　zhèng
Disease, illness.

癲(癫)　diān
Mentally deranged; insane.

癢(痒)　yǎng
Itchy, ticklish.

疲　pǐ
Tired, weary, exhausted.

疼　téng
Ache, pain, sore; love
dearly, dote on.

痛　tòng
Ache, pain; sadness;
extremely.

瘤　liú
Tumour.

痰　tán
Phlegm, sputum.

瘋（疯）fēng
Mad, insane, crazy.

痘　dòu
Smallpox.

痕　hén
Mark, trace; scar.

瘡（疮）chuāng
Sore, skin ulcer; wound.

痴　chī
Silly, idiotic; crazy
about; insane, mad.

瘦　shòu
Thin, emaciated;
infertile, poor.

疤　bā
Scar.

yāo

slender

RADICAL 52

么 , 'slender', manifests itself in a character like 幼, which pertains to youthfulness. Putting 么 beside 力, strength, the meaning comes across as 'to possess small strength'. And in 幽, the radical appears twice nestled inside a frame, reinforcing the meaning of 'secret' or 'hidden'.

幼

幻 huàn
Imaginary, illusory; magical, changeable.

幼 yòu
Young, underage; children, the young.

幽 yōu
Deep and remote; secret, hidden; quiet; imprison; of the nether world.

lǎo

old

RADICAL 125

Although the contemporary meaning of 考 is 'to examine' or 'to investigate', in the past it also meant 'aged', 'longevity', 'ancestors'. The former meanings have become obsolete, but the character still bears the 'old' radical. 者 being an auxiliary noun, carries no intrinsic meaning.

考 kǎo
Give or take a test or quiz; check, inspect; investigate, verify.

者 zhě
Auxiliary noun – that which is, who is. Referring to a person.

歹

dǎi

bad

RADICAL 78

Because the character originally written on shell is in the shape of a skeleton and a broken fragment of bone, the notion of death and destruction marks the majority of the examples. These include 殄 (exterminate), 殉 (sacrifice one's life), 殮 (put one's body into a coffin), 殃 (disaster).

殞

殘(残) cán
Incomplete, deficient; remnant; injure, damage; savage, cruel.

殞(殒) yǔn
Perish, die.

死 sǐ
Die; deadly; rigid, inflexible; impassable.

NUMERALS

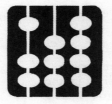

yī

one

RADICAL 1

Radicals under categories of Numerals and Basic Strokes do not provide a meaning to the characters listed under them. What has happened is that those characters which do not come under any other radical are classified here. For example, 上 and 下 , 世 , 丁 , all share the horizontal stroke, and are put willy-nilly under the 'one' radical.

丁　dīng
Man; family members, population; the fourth of the ten Heavenly Stems; fourth.

且　qiě
Just; for a long time; even; both.

上 shàng
Up; higher, superior;
first (part); go up; go
to; enter; apply.

下 xià
Below, under, down;
lower, inferior; next,
second; descend; take
away.

世 shì
Life, lifetime; age,
era; generation;
world.

丙 bǐng
The third of the ten
Heavenly Stems; third.

丑 chǒu
The second of the
twelve Earthly
Branches; clown.

丢 diū
Lose; throw; put aside.

bā

eight

RADICAL 12

Eight also performs as a radical because several characters possessing two downward strokes resemble the character for 'eight'. These two strokes are often found at the bottom, but as in 公 it is also written on top.

具

其 qí
His, her, its, their; that, such.

具 jù
Utensil, tool; possess, have; provide; a measure word.

字典

典　diǎn
Standard, law; literary quotation; ceremony; mortgage.

兼　jiān
Double; twice; simultaneously.

冀　jì
Hope, long for.

公共

公　gōng
Public; common, general; impartial; official business; male.

共　gòng
Common, general; share; together; altogether.

兮　xī
A gale has risen and is sweeping in clouds across the sky.

兵

兵　bīng
Weapons, arms; soldier; army, troops; military.

六　liù
Six.

shí

ten

RADICAL 24

The general 十 shape present in this group of characters justifies their belonging to this radical. In the case of 博 and 協 , the horizontal stroke is shrunk, and forms the left part of the character.

升

升 shēng
Rise, ascend; promote.

午 wǔ
Noon, midday; the seventh of the twelve Earthly Branches.

半

博

卓

卑　bēi
Low; inferior; modest.

半　bàn
Half; in the middle;
very little; partly.

卉　huì
Various kinds of grass.

千　qiān
Thousand; a great
number of.

协（協）xié
Joint, common; assist.

南　nán
South.

博　bó
Rich, abundant; win,
gain.

卅　sà
Thirty.

卓　zhuō
Tall and erect; eminent,
distinguished, outstan-
ding.

èr

two

RADICAL 7

The two horizontal strokes are incorporated in the character 井, whilst in others like 亞 and 互, they form the two horizontal boundaries. 五 is also classified under the 'two' radical.

互 hù
Mutual, each other.

井 jǐng
Well; pit, mine; neat, orderly.

亞(亚) yà
Inferior; second.

BASIC STROKES

RADICAL 4

A stroke slanting downwards to the left, this radical has belonging to it such a variety of characters like 久 and 乘. The downward stroke, however, does not always appear at the same angle.

乘

 ×

=

久 jiǔ
For a long time; how long?

乖 guāi
Well-behaved, good; clever, alert.

乘 chéng
Ride; take advantage of; multiply.

乙 yǐ

乙

RADICAL 5

し

乙 in its variant form is a downward stroke with a little hook at the end. It offers no distinct meaning, although the ancient shell form is of a meandering river.

亂

乙 yǐ
The second of the ten Heavenly Stems; second.

亂(乱) luàn
In disorder; chaos, turmoil; confused; random.

乾(干) gān
Dry; empty.

APPENDIX

Pinyin	Simplified	Regular	Meaning
qīng		清	clear
qíng		情	feelings
qíng		晴	fine weather
qíng	（请）	請	ask
jīng		睛	eyeball
jīng		精	excellent
juān		圈	surround
juàn		倦	tired
juǎn		捲	roll up
zhǎng	（涨）	漲	rise
zhàng	（帐）	帳	tent
zhàng	（账）	賬	account
zhàng	（胀）	脹	expand
hāi		咳	oh!
hái		孩	child
hái		骸	body
hài	（骇）	駭	startled
gāi	（该）	該	should
gāi	（赅）	賅	prepared
hé	（阂）	閡	obstacle
jiǎn	（俭）	儉	thrifty
jiǎn	（捡）	撿	gather
jiǎn	（检）	檢	examine

Pinyin	Simplified	Regular	Meaning
hěn		很	very
hěn		狠	cruel
hèn		恨	hate
gēn		根	root
gēn		跟	follow
hén		痕	scar
yín	（银）	銀	silver
yín	（龈）	齦	gum
bān		扳	pull
bǎn		坂	slope
bǎn		板	plank
bǎn		版	edition
bǎn	（钣）	鈑	metal sheet
fàn	（饭）	飯	rice
fàn	（贩）	販	trade
fǎn		返	return
biāo	（骠）	驃	cream-coloured horse
biāo	（镖）	鏢	dart
biāo		膘	fat of a stock animal
biāo	（标）	標	sign
biào	（鳔）	鰾	air bladders of fishes

Pinyin	Simplified	Regular	Meaning
bǎng		榜	example
bǎng		膀	upper arms
bàng		傍	near
bàng		磅	weighing scale
bàng	（谤）	謗	defame
bàng	（镑）	鎊	pound sterling
bāo		孢	spore
bāo		胞	placenta
bāo		炮	roast
bāo		苞	bract
bāo	（龅）	龅	protruding teeth
báo		雹	hail
bào		抱	embrace
bǎo	（饱）	飽	full
bào	（鲍）	鮑	abalone
bào		刨	to lend
pào		泡	foam
pào		炮	firecrackers
pǎo		跑	run
pǎo		袍	gown
biān	（编）	編	weave
biān	（鳊）	鯿	carp
biān		蝙	bat
biān		匾	tablet
biàn		遍	all over

Pinyin	Simplified	Regular	Meaning
bīn	（傧）	儐	entertain
bīn	（滨）	濱	beach
bīn	（缤）	繽	in confusion
bīng	（槟）	檳	areca-nut palm
bìn	（摈）	擯	reject
bìn	（膑）	臏	kneecap
bìn	（殡）	殯	carry to burial
bìn	（鬓）	鬢	hair on temples
zhī	（织）	織	knit
zhí	（职）	職	duty
zhì	（帜）	幟	banner
shí	（识）	識	know
fāng		坊	lane
fáng		妨	hinder
fāng	（钫）	鈁	francium
fāng		芳	fragrant
fáng		防	protect
fáng		肪	fat
fáng		房	dwelling
fǎng		仿	similar
fǎng	（访）	訪	visit
fàng		放	release

Pinyin	Simplified	Regular	Meaning
huī	（辉）	輝	shine
huī	（挥）	揮	wave
huī	（晖）	暉	ray of sunlight
hún	（浑）	渾	turbid
jī	（讥）	譏	ridicule
jī	（叽）	嘰	chirp
jī	（机）	機	machine
jī	（饥）	饑	hungry
jiǎo		狡	crafty
jiǎo	（饺）	餃	dumplings
jiǎo	（绞）	絞	twist
jiǎo		皎	clear
jiāo		郊	outskirts
xiào		校	school
xiào		效	effect
jué		決	decide
jué	（诀）	訣	bid farewell
jué		抉	choose
kuài		快	swift
zhuān	（砖）	磚	brick
zhuān	（转）	轉	revolve
chuán	（传）	傳	transfer

Pinyin	Simplified	Regular	Meaning
chāo		抄	copy
chāo	（钞）	鈔	paper money
chǎo		吵	disturb
chǎo		炒	fry
shā	（纱）	紗	yarn
shā		砂	gravel
shā		沙	sand
shā	（鲨）	鯊	shark
cuì		悴	sad
cuì		啐	spit
cuì		淬	to dip into water
cuì		粹	pure
cuì		萃	grassy
cuì		翠	bluish-green
cuì		瘁	care-worn
cuì		碎	fragmented
yáng	（扬）	揚	raise
yáng	（杨）	楊	aspen
yáng	（疡）	瘍	tumour
yáng	（阳）	陽	sun
fēng	（枫）	楓	maple
fēng	（疯）	瘋	insane
fēng	（讽）	諷	ridicule
sà	（飒）	颯	sound of wind blowing through the trees

Pinyin	Simplified	Regular	Meaning
lóng	（枕）	櫳	cage
lóng	（茏）	龍	lush
lóng	（笼）	籠	basket
lóng	（聋）	聾	deaf
lǒng	（扰）	攏	assemble
lǒng	（垄）	壟	rice-field
lún	（伦）	倫	logic
lún	（抡）	掄	select
lún	（轮）	輪	wheel
lún	（沦）	淪	sink
lún	（纶）	綸	fishing-line
màn	（谩）	謾	disrespectful
màn		漫	overflow
màn		慢	slow
màn		幔	curtain
màn		蔓	creeper
mán	（鳗）	鰻	eel
mán	（馒）	饅	steamed bread
lán	（兰）	蘭	orchid
lán	（拦）	攔	block
lán	（栏）	欄	railing
lán	（谰）	讕	slander
lán	（澜）	瀾	strong waves
làn	（烂）	爛	overcooked

Pinyin	Simplified	Regular	Meaning
gōu	（沟）	溝	creek
gòu	（构）	構	build
gòu	（购）	購	buy
gòu	（觏）	覯	meet
gòu		媾	make peace
hú	（胡）	鬍	beard
hú		湖	lake
hú		蝴	butterfly
hú		糊	paste
hú		葫	gourd
huáng		惶	terrified
huáng		煌	luminous
huáng		蝗	locust
huáng		湟	leisure
wān		剜	cut out
wān		蜿	meander
wǎn		惋	pity
wǎn		婉	obliging
wǎn		碗	bowl
wàn		腕	wrist
lù	（录）	錄	record
lù	（绿）	綠	green
lù	（碌）	碌	busy

Pinyin	Simplified	Regular	Meaning
mō		摸	touch
mó	（馍）	馍	dumplings
mó		模	pattern
mó		膜	membrane
mò		漠	desert
mò		貘	tapir
mò		寞	silent
mò		瘼	sufferings
liāo		撩	raise
liáo		僚	official
liáo		撩	disturb
liáo		嘹	resonant
liáo		燎	set ablaze
liáo		寮	hut
liáo	（缭）	繚	encircle
liáo	（疗）	療	cure
liáo	（辽）	遼	far
liǎo		潦	scribble
liǎo	（了）	瞭	understand
liào	（镣）	鐐	shackles
quán	（颧）	顴	cheekbones
quán	（权）	權	authority
quàn	（劝）	勸	encourage
huān	（欢）	歡	cheerful

Pinyin	Simplified	Regular	Meaning
ráo	（娆）	嬈	graceful
ráo	（饶）	饒	abundant
rào	（绕）	繞	entwine
shāo	（烧）	燒	burn
xiǎo	（晓）	曉	dawn
xiá	（侠）	俠	hero
xiá	（狭）	狹	narrow
xiá	（峡）	峽	gorge
xié	（挟）	挾	clamp
péi		陪	accompany
péi		培	cultivate
péi	（赔）	賠	compensate
táng		塘	embankment
táng		搪	keep out
táng		糖	sweets
táng		溏	pond
zēng		增	multiply
zēng		憎	detest
zèng	（赠）	贈	offer

Pinyin	Simplified	Regular	Meaning
zhēng		挣	struggle
zhēng		狰	ferocious
zhēng		峥	steep
zhēng	（铮）	錚	metallic clang
zhēng		箏	string instrument
tōng		通	passable
tǒng		桶	bucket
tǒng		捅	poke
tòng		痛	pain
tān	（摊）	攤	spread
tān	（滩）	灘	beach
tān	（瘫）	癱	paralyse
lí		狸	fox
lí		厘	unit of measure
lǐ		俚	rude
lǐ		理	structure
lǐ	（鲤）	鯉	carp
mái		埋	bury

Pinyin	Simplified	Regular	Meaning
tāi		胎	embryo
tái		抬	lift
tái		苔	moss
tái	（台）	颱	typhoon
shǐ		始	beginning
huǐ		悔	regret
huì		晦	dark
huì	（诲）	誨	teach
hǎi		海	sea
méi		梅	plum
méi		酶	yeast
qiàn		歉	bad harvest
qiàn		慊	hateful
xián		嫌	suspicion
fān		幡	streamers
fān		翻	turn over
fán		蕃	luxuriant
fán		璠	a jade
fán		燔	roast
fán		蹯	paws
pán		蟠	coil

Pinyin	Simplified	Regular	Meaning
kū		枯	withered
kū		骷	skeleton
kǔ		苦	bitter
gū		估	estimate
gū		咕	coo
gū		沽	buy and sell
gū		姑	aunt
gū		酤	wine
gū		辜	crime
gū	（诂）	詁	layman terms
gù		牯	cow
gù		固	firm
gù		痼	bad habit
tī		梯	ladder
tì		剃	shave
tì		涕	mucus
dì		睇	look askance
dì		第	position
mēng	（蒙）	矇	deceive
méng		獴	mongoose
méng		檬	lemon
méng		朦	misty

Pinyin	Simplified	Regular	Meaning
láo	（劳）	勞	labour
láo	（唠）	嘮	nag
láo	（痨）	癆	tuberculosis
lāo	（捞）	撈	dredge
láng		狼	wolf
láng		琅	a jade
láng		郎	gentleman
láng		廊	verandah
lǎng		朗	bright
làng		浪	waves
gěng		哽	choke
gěng	（绠）	綆	rope attached to a bucket
gěng		梗	stem
gěng	（鲠）	鯁	fish-bone
dīng	（钉）	釘	nail
dīng		盯	watch closely
dīng		叮	inquire into
dìng	（订）	訂	arrange
qiáo		憔	haggard
qiáo		樵	firewood
qiáo		瞧	look

Pinyin	Simplified	Regular	Meaning
fén	（坟）	墳	grave
fén	（渍）	濆	highland alongside a river
fèn	（偾）	僨	ruin
fèn	（愤）	憤	anger
jùn		俊	handsome
jùn		峻	steep
jùn	（骏）	駿	noble steed
jùn		竣	finish
suō		唆	instigate
suō		梭	weaving shuttle
quān		悛	repent
ráng		瓤	pulp
rǎng		壤	soil
rǎng		攘	reject
rǎng		嚷	yell
ràng	（让）	讓	make way
shēn		伸	stretch
shēn		呻	groan
shēn	（绅）	紳	gentry
shēn		砷	arsenic
shén		神	God

Pinyin	Simplified	Regular	Meaning
tiāo		佻	frivolous
tiāo		挑	choose
tiào		眺	gaze
tiào		跳	jump
tiāo		窕	refined
yáo	(谣)	謠	ballad
yáo	(徭)	徭	forced labour
yáo	(摇)	搖	shake
yáo	(瑶)	瑤	beautiful jade
zǎo		澡	bathe
zào		噪	make noise
zào		燥	dry
zào		躁	impatient
zhōng	(钟)	鍾	goblet
zhōng	(肿)	腫	swollen
zhòng	(种)	種	grow
zhǒng		踵	heal
xiáng	(详)	詳	thorough
yáng		佯	pretend
yáng		洋	ocean
yǎng		氧	oxygen

Pinyin	Simplified	Regular	Meaning
zhū	（朱）	硃	scarlet
zhū		侏	dwarf
zhū	（诛）	誅	execute
zhū		珠	pearl
zhū		株	exposed roots of a tree
zhū		蛛	spider
zhù		住	stay
zhù		注	notice
zhù	（驻）	駐	be stationed
zhù		柱	pillar
zhù		蛀	decay
zū		租	rent
zǔ	（诅）	詛	curse
zǔ		阻	obstruct
zǔ	（组）	組	organize
zǔ		祖	ancestors
jǔ		沮	stop
jǔ		咀	chew
jiě		姐	sister
cū		粗	rough
kǎo		拷	flog
kǎo		烤	roast
kào	（铐）	銬	handcuff

Pinyin	Simplified	Regular	Meaning
dú	（独）	獨	solitary
zhú	（烛）	燭	candle
chù	（触）	觸	touch
zhuó	（浊）	濁	muddy
zhuó	（镯）	鐲	bracelet
zhāo		招	beckon
shào		劭	exhort
shào	（绍）	紹	continue
zhāo		昭	obvious
zhāo		沼	pond
zhào	（诏）	詔	instruct
diāo		貂	sable
pǐ		劈	split
pǐ		癖	addiction
pì		僻	secluded
pì		譬	analogy
pǐ		霹	thunderbolt
kǎn		砍	chop
chuī		吹	blow
kǎn		坎	ridge
yǐn	（饮）	飲	drink
chuī		炊	cook

Pinyin	Simplified	Regular	Meaning
tuó	（驼）	駝	camel
tuó	（鸵）	鴕	ostrich
tuó		陀	a top
duò		舵	rudder
hè		褐	coarse cloth
hè		喝	drink
kě		渴	thirsty
gé		葛	creeping plant
mù		募	solicit
mù		墓	tomb
mù		幕	tent
mù		暮	dusk
mù		慕	admire
méi		媒	matchmaker
méi		煤	coal
móu	（谋）	謀	strategy
tíng		蜓	dragonfly
tíng		霆	thunderclap
tíng		庭	courtyard
tǐng		挺	stick up
tǐng		艇	small boat

Pinyin	Simplified	Regular	Meaning
jiǎ		假	false
xiá		瑕	red stain on a jade
xiá		暇	leisure
xiá		霞	rosy clouds
xiá		遐	distant
xiā	（虾）	蝦	prawn
zhān		沾	moisten
zhàn		站	stand
zhān		粘	paste
tie	（贴）	貼	allowance
tiē		帖	invitation
tóng		桐	tung tree
tóng	（铜）	銅	bronze
tóng		筒	tube-shaped container
dòng		峒	cave
dòng		恫	threaten
dòng		洞	hole
dòng		胴	large intestines

飽跑電苞泡